THE MINIATURE HOUSE

THE MINIATURE HOUSE

FAITH EATON

PHOTOGRAPHS BY NICK NICHOLSON

HARRY N. ABRAMS, INC., PUBLISHERS

NEW YORK

Text copyright © 1990 Faith Eaton
Photographs copyright (except for those on p. 160) © Weidenfeld & Nicolson Ltd 1990
Published in 1991 by Harry N. Abrams, Incorporated, New York
A Times Mirror Company
All rights reserved.
No part of the contents of this book may be reproduced without the written permission of the publisher

Library of Congress Cataloging-in-Publication Data

Eaton, Faith.
    The miniature house/Faith Eaton.
      p. cm.
    Includes bibliographical references.
    ISBN 0-8109-3608-9
    1. Doll-houses—History.   2. Miniature dolls—History.   I. Title
NK4893. E34 1990
745.592′3—dc20   90-352 CIP

Endpapers   *West Wood House. See page 89.*

Frontispiece   *Nursery in a burgher's house from the eighteenth-century German court of Mon Plaisir. See page 29.*

Page 8   *On this drumtop table in a corner of Mrs Carlisle's Chippendale Library are the two books described on page 129 and some of the smallest miniature books in her collection.*

Page 15   *This fully-equipped and well-staffed kitchen in Princess Augusta Dorothea's Mon Plaisir provides a fascinating record of life below stairs in an early eighteenth-century German palace.*

Printed and bound in Italy

CONTENTS

To the makers of miniatures, past and present, whose small creations give such enormous pleasure . . . *whatsoever things are lovely . . . if there be any praise, think on these things.*

St Paul

ACKNOWLEDGEMENTS

During the production of this book it was necessary to visit five countries and the author would like to acknowledge, with gratitude, the kindness and help so readily given by all who were approached for assistance during research and photographic sessions.

Most appreciative thanks for his co-operation are due to Nick Nicholson, whose photographs form an integral and important part of this book and whose unfailing patience and good humour deserve special mention.

Caroline Goodfellow is especially thanked for all her help – particularly with the typescript – and for generously supplying some extra photographs of Mon Plaisir. As always, she, and the entire staff at the Bethnal Green Museum of Childhood, were extremely helpful. My thanks also go to Michal Morse for invaluable help proof-reading.

Other people in England who kindly supplied vital information and who deserve particular thanks are: Mrs Diana Gray, Mrs Carlisle's daughter, whose gracious co-operation in providing biographical details and family photographs of her mother was invaluable; the owner of West Wood House, who most kindly allowed it to be included in and specially photographed for this book; and David West, the maker of the house, who was most helpful and generously supplied essential information and extra photographs.

Grateful thanks are also given to Jill Bennett, Charlotte Zeepvat and The Dolls' House, Covent Garden, for necessary information, and to Mrs Pam Whittaker of the National Trust, Mrs Joy Ramsay, conservator, and Mr and Mrs Gillett, administrators at Nunnington; also to three people in particular at Weidenfeld and Nicolson, Suzannah Gough, Emma Way and Jenny Wilson.

In France most appreciative thanks to go the Musée des Arts Décoratifs, Paris, for permission to photograph exhibits, and especially to Madame Barbara Spadaccini-Day for all her kindness and assistance; and to the Musée des Arts et Traditions Populaires, Paris, for permission to take photographs, with additional thanks to Madame Anne Marie Kefi and her assistant when photographing items in store.

In Holland grateful thanks are given to the Gemeentemuseum, der Haag, for permission to photograph Sara Ploos van Amstel's cabinet house, with particular thanks to Peter Couvee. Also to the Frans Hals Museum, Haarlem, for their kind assistance over photographs of Sara Ploos van Amstel's second cabinet house and her portrait.

In the Deutsch Democratik Republik many thanks are given to the Minister für Kültur, Herr Schubert and his staff, particularly Fraülein Annette Weiska, also to the Cultural Attaché at the British Embassy in East Berlin, Iaian Frater, for his kind assistance.

Thanks are given to the Museum der Stadt Arnstadt, Thüringia, for permission to photograph Mon Plaisir and to the Direktor, Herr Kästner and his staff, with particularly grateful thanks to Herr Matteus Klein. Also to the Deutsches Spielzeugmuseum, Sonneberg, for permission to use their library with most grateful thanks to the Direktor, Herr Gauss and his very helpful staff.

In the United States of America thanks are given to the Museum of Science and Industry Chicago for permission to photograph Colleen Moore's Fairy Castle, with particularly appreciative thanks for their kindness and help to Ioan Boca, Keith Gill, Mrs Veronica Robertson and Miss Pat Kennedy; also to the Art Institute of Chicago for their permission and help over the Thorne Rooms' photographs with particular thanks to Miss Karen McLean Johnson.

FOREWORD

Thirty-five years ago, when my first antique dolls' house arrived to join two childhood treasures which were new in the 1930s, few books even mentioned the subject though to collectors' delight, two tra1-blazers, Vivien Greene's scholarly *English Dolls' Houses of the eighteenth and nineteenth centuries* and Flora Gill Jacob's comprehensive *History of Dolls' Houses*, had just been published. Now collectors' shelves hold an ever increasing assortment of books about dolls' houses covering their history, how to collect, conserve and even make them.

Although, hopefully, this book may find a place beside such volumes it is not, strictly speaking, about dolls' houses at all: for want of a better collective noun to describe such a varied group the examples featured in these pages have been gathered together under the heading *The Miniature House*.

And when is a miniature house not a doll's house? Without in any way wishing to appear pedantic there is a considerable difference between the two descriptions, even though any strict line of demarkation may be somewhat blurred on occasion.

As soon as any rule is made the first illustrations that spring to mind are usually the exceptions to it: so let it be suggested, purely as a guide rather than a dividing line, that dolls' houses are more often than not connected with children's play and may be commercially or sometimes even crudely made, whereas miniature and baby houses, with their fine elaborate interiors, were most likely made for adults, who wished to display tiny objets d'art in a suitably realistic setting, and which often recorded styles of furnishing and interior decoration fashionable at that time.

Miniature houses may be discovered within cabinets and cupboards or be replicas of real houses; but baby houses and dolls' houses are almost invariably 'buildings' rather than pieces of furniture. (By this definition the miniature house given to young Ann Sharp by her godmother, Princess Anne, in 1695, should not be called a baby house; but, as has been pointed out already, there are always exceptions to every rule and this time-honoured name is frequently used instead of the descriptive cupboard-house.)

Mon Plaisir, the miniature representation of Princess Augusta Dorothea von Schwarzburg-Arnstadt's court, town and neighbourhood, was made for her in the eighteenth century, although now contained in cases it is unique, and is the supreme and unsurpassed example of the extent to which a passion for collecting miniatures and recording daily life can go. During that century many cultured and affluent women collected small replicas and displayed them in fine miniature houses in their homes. In England these miniature houses were referred to as baby houses as the term then, of course, meant 'little', (in the same way they used another word 'toy'). Such baby houses were displayed in reception rooms, or perhaps a hall or landing, in large houses where the ladies could enjoy these collectors' items; the examples at Nostell Priory and Uppark are probably the two finest and best-known English baby houses.

In Holland and Germany from the seventeenth century onwards wealthy women often made a serious study of contemporary fashion and decor and reproduced them on dolls and in miniature houses. Many of the German houses had realistic interiors and, though most of the fronts were open to view, the exterior sides, roofs and backs copied full-size houses.

Some examples may have been used as teaching-toys by mothers intent on instilling housewifery skills into their young daughters, but all were adults' possessions and kept well away from the unsupervised young.

Some German, and more Dutch eighteenth-century women, like Sara Ploos van Amstel, converted the interiors of beautiful cabinets in their reception rooms into cabinet houses, thus having the double pleasure of looking at fine pieces of full-size furniture when their doors were closed, and at houses full of miniature treasures when they were open.

Because few, if any, eighteenth-century children were as fortunate as little Ann Sharp it was not until the second half of the nineteenth century that dolls' houses were commonly found in English nurseries.

Once such things were commercially made they became playthings; the name dolls' house was then both descriptive and apt and the old term, baby house, fell out of fashion. In the same way, in Germany, the earlier miniature house, which delighted adults, was a *dockenhaus* and the later term, *puppenhaus* (which equated to the English dolls' house), was used for all miniature houses once children were permitted to enjoy their own versions.

During the nineteenth century dolls' houses were increasingly popular and sometimes, in particularly fine examples, women carried on the tradition of the baby house and filled even commercially made ones with valuable miniatures.

However, the renaissance of the grand, palatial baby house occurred, unexpectedly, in the 1920s and 1930s, when Titania's Palace and Queen Mary's Dolls' House were created in England and the Fairy Castle was designed for the film star Colleen Moore in the United States of America. At the same time two collectors, Mrs Carlisle and Mrs Thorne, one in England and the other in America, were inspired to create sets of miniature rooms.

Recently, with the revival of interest in fine miniature craftsmanship, collectors have been able to commission exquisite pieces of work and, again, create miniature stately homes; the second renaissance this century of the baby house is taking place now, and West Wood House is one splendid example in England.

In this book not all of the examples contain dolls, not all are shaped like traditional baby houses, but all were created by and for adult collectors and each one exemplifies, in its own particular way, the fascination of a miniature house and its treasures.

Introduction

A museum, where men in uniform stand guard in vast halls full of untouchable things, could seem a boring or even frigtening place to a very young child. However, from the first visit, when knee-high if not to a grasshopper at least to the legs of most showcases, museums were to me enchanted palaces. My father, having the incomparable gift of being able to see with the eyes of a child and plan with the wisdom of age, was inspired to make that first visit to Lancaster House, then the old London Museum. His insistence that we did not stop to look at anything as we walked past case after case was puzzling but, finally, at the end of a little passage in the basement we did stop and he lifted me up to look at the only thing which he had brought me to see that day, a tiny silver teaset on a miniature silver tray.

To single out one small exhibit in that enormous collection for such attention was, as he had meant it to be, an unforgettable experience, for which my gratitude is eternal as a lifetime of being enthralled by miniatures has meant not only the unending fascination of studying the objects themselves, but the pleasure of meeting many interesting people during travels and research.

Who made the miniatures, who collected them, why, how and when have always formed part of their enticing appeal, so the decision of which miniature houses to select for this book really was made for me by their owners and makers.

The provenance of both sets of rooms and three of the four houses chosen was not only accessible but most fully documented; and to be able to record the maker relating how the fourth example, West Wood House, was made was a sheer delight.

To none of these collectors was their miniature creation merely a pastime to while away hours of leisure; all six women were actively involved, over a period of many years, in projects which had for each of them a very definite purpose.

The choice of the two eighteenth-century examples and the leap forward into the twentieth century for the others was determined by the links between them, as since 1900 there have been two renaissance periods, as it were, for houses created in the manner of the earlier century when such things were designed by adults for adult enjoyment.

There are also more personal links; certainly in five of the projects described here (and probably in the sixth) there are items made specifically for them by their owners, a book or piece of furniture, carpets and rugs, embroidery and dolls' clothes, paintings and three-dimensional plants; all have been designed and made by these talented as well as dedicated collectors.

To describe the German Princess Augusta Dorothea von Schwarzburg-Arnstadt as a dedicated collector is to give a truthful, though scarcely adequate description. This remarkable woman, born six years after Charles II was restored to the English throne, was for all of her adult life an avid and wildly extravagant collector. Being the daughter of the Duke Anton von Braunschweig-Wolfenbüttel (who was renowned for his art collection) it was not surprising that she also should be a collector and wish to have a fine porcelain room, picture gallery and valuable objets d'art in her palace of the Augustenburg. Regrettably, she emptied the coffers not only of her own exchequer but also that of her husband, borrowed large sums of money from relatives and was in debt long before the palace could be completed according to her ambitious designs.

Perhaps she turned her attention from her full-size palace to the creation of the miniature, and most aptly named, Mon Plaisir in a desperate attempt, literally, to minimize her spending.

However, she was inspired to recreate in miniature not only her court but the nearby town of Arnstadt and the surrounding countryside; an achievement which involved court ladies, a convent of nuns and craftsmen throughout the principality in the making of over four hundred dolls and two thousand six hundred miniature items to go into all the buildings and streets, so as an exercise in economy it was hardly the most effective way to save money.

To see Mon Plaisir for the necessary research and photography meant visiting the Deutsch Democratik Republik. On each of the two occasions it so happened that the expeditions had to be made in icy mid-winter, not the easiest time to drive through the mountainous region of Thüringia in eastern Germany, where Arnstadt and the nearby 'toy-towns' of Sonneberg and Waltershausen are located.

The Stadt Museum of Arnstadt has many treasures to display, and that it has allocated seven large rooms to show the component parts of Mon Plaisir indicates the regard in which this amazing miniature complex is held.

To stand in the first room and look straight through the doorways of the other six in the wing beyond and realize all their cases contain exhibits from one eighteenth-century woman's project is an awe-inspiring experience. Mon Plaisir is a microcosm which, if we wish, has the power to transport us back two hundred and sixty years into the environment of the Princess and all the people who helped her to preserve their 'world' in this miniature time-capsule.

The Dutch collector, Sara Ploos van Amstel, was born in 1699 (thirty-three years after Princess Augusta Dorothea) and for some years their projects overlapped. She, too, was concerned with reproducing accurately the environment in which she lived and, though her achievement cannot compare in size or scope with that of the Princess, she has left us a priceless glimpse into two eighteenth-century homes, for her rooms are realistically and far more fully furnished than those we see today in Mon Plaisir.

Although Sara Ploos van Amstel limited her record to two affluent Dutch households their interior decoration is elaborate and the contents of very fine quality. Many of the silver and porcelain miniatures in the rooms are valuable in their own right, so her cabinet-houses are not only small-scale reproductions of contemporary homes but also display-cases for collectors' miniatures.

As both these eighteenth-century women were intent on recording daily-life in their own time and place it would be fascinating to know how they would react to the third collector's project. The Fairy Castle created for the American film star, Colleen Moore, early in this century is the realization of her childhood invention, when she imagined clouds to be ethereal palaces. It is as far removed from reality as any building anywhere over the rainbow could be, a visible fantasy designed for invisible inhabitants.

Arguably it is more suitable for such occupants than the English Palace built for Titania by Sir Neville Wilkinson: beautiful and valuable though that costly miniature building is it lacks the Castle's shimmering quality and the humorous touches displayed so often by its designers. The library in the Castle, with some chairs and couches specially designed for the comfort of people with wings, the great hall with its vertigo-inducing staircase (which is, of course, perfectly acceptable to anyone capable of flying up and down if they preferred), these are only two of the imaginative features which produce the required ethereal quality and add a pleasing, if unexpected, touch of humour.

Two more features, which lift the Castle out of the 'Hollywood Tinsel' category and make it a fitting building for Lewis Carroll's Alice to visit in Wonderland, are the beautifully painted murals and the decorative panels framing so many of the rooms.

The blend of humour and imagination, seen so often throughout the Castle, is vividly expressed in the library's decor and furniture for example, and just suggested by the sparkling delicacy of the cobweb quilt on the Princess's bed.

Colleen Moore was actively involved in the making of the Castle as she, like Mrs Thorne, searched in Europe as well as America over a period of many years for the miniature antiques of ivory, silver and precious stones that she wished to place inside it; she also wrote the story of *The Enchanted Castle* which is in the library.

A fairy-tale castle constructed by two Hollywood set designers, which appeals to any imaginative child and to all adults who appreciate exquisite miniature antiques in a beautiful, fantastic setting, is a creation worthy of careful study as well as light-hearted appreciation.

Rather more down to earth and equally fascinating is the miniature house, West Wood, which is a superb piece of modern craftsmanship in the style of a traditional English baby house, but designed with original and imaginative touches. They are more subtle than those displayed in the fairy-tale castle, as might be expected in an English real life replica, but they do prolong and increase the viewer's pleasure and interest in this thirty-roomed miniature country house.

There is another link with the ethereal as the owner, saddened by the removal of Titania's Palace from its native soil to Denmark's Legoland after its auction in 1978, consoled herself with the idea of having a special miniature house of her own and found the artist who, for several years off and on, worked to design and create this most unusual and desirable residence.

She herself during this time followed in the footsteps of Sara Ploos van Amstel and Mrs Thorne and collected antique and commissioned new miniature items for the house; she also made many of the beautiful carpets, paintings and tiny flowering plants for West Wood.

In all these miniature homes there is a mixture of antique and specially commissioned items and they all have a more unusual feature in common, their exceptionally fine painted walls. The decorative panels in Mon Plaisir, the lovely landscape scenes in the Dutch cabinet house, the fairy-tale murals in Colleen Moore's Castle and the wall paintings in West Wood are all beautiful examples of the ways artists in the eighteenth and twentieth centuries have embellished miniature rooms.

Painted walls, decorative and scenic, also attracted Mrs Thorne and many of the full-size rooms which inspired her to create particular examples in her miniature series have such decorative features. Mrs Carlisle as well as Mrs Thorne was inspired to make a set of rooms in the 1920s and 1930s. Both collectors commissioned some of the finest craftsmen specializing in miniature work and their projects, though created for very different reasons, perfectly suggest the ambiance of the periods they represent.

Like the earlier collectors Mrs Thorne wanted to capture and present a certain period's appearance and 'feel' in every miniature room she created. Her aim was serious, though she enjoyed every moment, for she wished to provide an instructive record of the major influences of interior design in the United States of America and in Europe from the seventeenth century.

During her lifetime of extensive travelling she found antique miniatures and commissioned craftsmen abroad as well as in the United States of America, where she had a studio for the team assembling the rooms she planned.

Like the Princess Augusta Dorothea she was the mastermind, overseeing every aspect of her engrossing project. It was her own personal choice which decided which style the next room should illustrate, what (full-size) rooms best exemplified the essence of the effect she sought to recreate and which would serve as her inspiration for the miniature version, and, though she employed draughtsmen, artists and craftsmen, she supervised every step of the construction.

Though not as obsessional as the Princess she was certainly a dedicated collector, with a very firm resolve, not just to create beautiful room-settings for her own pleasure, but to use such visual aids to educate all those who were interested enough to view her series of rooms.

None of her rooms on display has any doll representing a human element in it. In some of the very first rooms that she created, and in the last few, she did include a few examples, but she felt that, for the 'important' rooms, designed for public viewing and not as gifts for family and friends, she could not provide dolls which matched the realistic quality of the settings. Instead she used, and only when she felt it to be appropriate, a book or some personal possession to suggest the room was part of a house and not, as was more frequently the case, a room in its own right, so to speak.

The rooms created by Mrs Carlisle are also unoccupied; but her feelings about dolls seem to have been stronger than those of Mrs Thorne, who just regretted none was up to the standard she felt she had achieved with the furniture and accessories. In reply to my enquiry as to why her mother had not included dolls in her rooms, Mrs Carlisle's daughter's reply was brief and to the point, 'She hated them!'

It was interesting to discover that, although Mrs Thorne and Mrs Carlisle seemed to be running on parallel lines regarding their projects, roughly over the same period and often employing the same craftsmen in England, their motives for collecting were entirely different and they never met or corresponded.

Unlike Mrs Thorne, who was thoroughly professional in her research of the subject and her use of it, Mrs Carlisle's rooms reflect her fascination for the needlework which was her lifelong absorbing interest, and also her more informal planning of the rooms. Many of them were inspired by incidents in her life (the nurseries, for instance, followed the birth of her grandchildren), or were built around one particular piece of furniture and all were separate entities, not part of a programmed sequence.

All the exquisitely made carpets, chairseats and other needlework these rooms contain were the work of Mrs Carlisle, so her involvement in the rooms' creation meant far more than their designing. Some time before she died she gave the rooms into the care of the National Trust and they can now be seen in one of the houses administered by the Trust, Nunnington Hall. This means that, of all the miniature houses and rooms described, only West Wood maintains the tradition of such houses as it stands in a prominent position downstairs in its owner's home.

The last chapter in the book concentrates on the inhabitants of miniature houses, the little dolls who can add so much to the rooms' interest, or completely ruin the realistic atmosphere which has been carefully set up with miniature furniture and accessories which are perfect replicas of full-size pieces.

Because collectors never cease to argue over the effect dolls can have many examples are shown, in a variety of rooms, so that readers can make up their own minds. When planning which illustrations to use it was fascinating (and rather unnerving) to realize, when looking a second time more closely into the details of the photographs, that many of the dolls which enhanced the 'realistic' look of elegant salons were not, in themselves, at all natural looking. For example, the illustration on page 153 shows a group of charmingly dressed occupants apparently listening to one member playing the harp in the drawing room of the house at Audley End. They add interest to the room as they represent exactly the kind of people who, in real life, occupied their leisure hours this way in many houses during the early nineteenth century, yet none of the little wooden dolls is in the least life-like. The amusing thing is so few people are immediately aware of this fact; the dolls appear to blend so well with their setting that the initial reaction is often to accept them without questioning their appearance.

On the other hand little bisque dolls with 'natural' faces can often irritate at first glance, usually because the stiffness of their attitude draws attention to the conflict between the realistic face and unnatural pose and spoils the very effect they were intended to convey. Maybe more than beauty being, 'in the eye of the beholder', it is how people react to different kinds of dolls in miniature houses which is as fascinating as the study of the dolls themselves.

Of course, in rooms where realism is not of prime importance, in the delightful dolls' houses which have a mixture of furniture and accessories in wildly different scales, the realistic quality of the dolls is of no importance, and the assortment of wax, wood and ceramic inhabitants often adds to the charm of the house.

In miniature houses, where adults have attempted to reproduce with perfect small-scale replicas rooms in full-scale houses, the situation is somewhat altered; and one can see why Mrs Thorne, for instance, chose to display her rooms unoccupied rather than introduce a jarring note to spoil their effective realism.

However, few would prefer to see Mon Plaisir unpopulated, and the equally fine wax dolls in Sara Ploos van Amstel's house would be sadly missed if they were removed from the cabinet.

Whether someone chooses to suggest the presence of occupants by leaving a pair of shoes by a bedside, to imagine the unseen inhabitants or to populate miniature households with a choice of whatever dolls are thought to be most suitable is up to every owner; and we can be thankful that there is this wide variety of presentation to choose from, for each choice links the owner to their possession in a very personal and individual way and that, in itself, adds much to the value of the miniature house.

One of the most satisfying sights today is to see small children looking attentively into cases containing dolls' houses and miniature rooms in museums specially designed for children's pleasure and education.

Sensible and imaginative parents (and teachers) can stimulate them into registering what they look at, by using stories or quizzes perhaps. For these little glimpses into kitchens and living-rooms of bygone days are far more than nostalgic pleasures for those of us enjoying 'second childhood'; they are the best teaching aids a young child can have to an appreciation of the way people of past generations lived in different countries.

Perhaps some of them will grow up to be so intrigued by the miniature world that their interest will result in research and friendships throughout the full-size one. May their enjoyment equal mine over as many years.

CHAPTER ONE

An Eighteenth-Century German Court: Mon Plaisir

The most dedicated collectors of miniatures would enjoy looking at the Museen der Stadt Arnstadt's full-size treasures, especially the porcelain and tapestries, but the magnet attracting them to this interesting place, deep in the Thüringian region of the eastern part of Germany, is Mon Plaisir.

Nobody knows its original design. It was planned by the Princess Augusta Dorothea von Schwarzburg-Arnstadt, in the early eighteenth century, as a miniature representation of her court and town, with streets of buildings in different scales and painted backcloths, but exactly how they were arranged is guesswork. Having a meticulous eye for authentic detail she probably followed, as closely as possible, the main plan of Arnstadt and the district at the time.

There is sometimes a confusion over her title as well as that of her project. Her husband, originally the Duke of Schwarzburg-Arnstadt, arranged the elevation of his state to a principality by a very costly agreement in 1697. From that date her title changed from Duchess to Princess (although some German writers always refer to her as Fürstin). As French was the official language in most European courts her model project was called Mon Plaisir rather than Mein Vergnügen.

Today, court, town and countryside are contained in eighty separate settings in glazed, white cases of different sizes, and they fill seven museum rooms. Over four hundred dolls, mostly ten inches tall, represent every strata of society from prince to pauper, in palatial rooms, workshops, streets, burgher's houses, convent and chapel, town and countryside.

Some cases are plain, with shelves holding four, six or eight settings, some are roofed to suggest houses while others are basic 'wings' of houses – for originally some of these structures were joined together to make realistic houses. The one illustrated opposite is approximately eight feet from floor to chimney-top, so the rooms are large scale. The two main rooms are described on pages 26–7 and 39; the two smaller ones on the lowest floor illustrate the elaborate toilette of a court lady seated at her dressing-table and, in an equally fine appartment, a courtier being shaved by his barber.

After the Princess's death in 1751 Erfurt's orphanage asked for Mon Plaisir, but delayed permission meant it was not moved until eleven years later; it was unsuccessfully auctioned in 1765 and then, after many discussions, lent to Arnstadt's orphanage in 1766. They made a little money by displaying it until 1850.

Its ownership was questioned several times but finally, in 1881, Princess Marie von Schwarzburg-Sondershausen claimed it. She repaired some damaged items and kept it in her palace until she gave it to the Museen der Stadt Arnstadt in 1930, when experts began restoring it.

During the 1939 war it was dismantled for safety and reinstalled there in the 1950s.

The whole concept of Mon Plaisir was an amazing one for anybody to organize, even if they could call upon every craftsman and needlewoman for miles around. That it has survived all the problems of disputed ownership, dismantling and resiting, damage, loss and a wartime evacuation in its nearly three-hundred years of existence is no less wonderful.

As Mon Plaisir illustrates so much of the daily life of her people during the time she lived in the Augustenburg, historians today owe much to the Princess for creating such a valuable record. Mon Plaisir is the equivalent of a whole series of documentary films seen in three dimensions, for Princess Augusta Dorothea's intention was to recreate in miniature the whole spectrum of society in appropriate sets.

She is unique in her field in this ambition; other collectors have given us a glimpse into a particular period house, but no one else has handed down such an amazing, comprehensive and authentic dossier.

PRINCESS AUGUSTA DOROTHEA

Judging by this illustration apparently Augusta Dorothea von Schwarzburg-Arnstadt lacked the gift of seeing herself as others saw her, for the doll (the making of which she supervised) certainly looks more attractive than her actual portrait.

Lacking positive identification it must be assumed these dolls represent the Prince and Princess: they appear together elsewhere (page 35) and the host-Prince again wears an identical yellow coat in the porcelain room (page 38); here he has added a dress-sword, gloves and tricorne hat.

The Princess, ensconced in some state upon an elaborately draped 'throne', wears a paler yellow costume trimmed with much silver lace. Her wig resembles a judge's, but does have ribbon trimming, and the whole effect is of ceremonial splendour.

The Princess doll has a rather determined facial expression, and the opulence of her throne, the Chinese wall-coverings, and the further exotic touch of a pet monkey, do betray rather than suggest the real Princess's extravagant tastes.

Probably unintentionally the Prince doll appears to be supplicating his formidable wife – probably remonstrating with her over continuous reckless spending.

It was her extravagance in real life that caused a rift, for their marriage seems to have begun happily enough.

Born in 1666 Augusta Dorothea was the daughter of Duke Ulrich II of Braunschweig-Wolfenbüttel who, when she was eighteen, married her to Anton Gunther II of Schwarzburg-Arnstadt. Unlike many aristocratic young girls she had met her husband already as he had been partly educated at her father's court.

Early in their marriage Anton Günther gave her some land near their palace of Käfernburg; Augusta Dorothea built her own palace, the Augustenburg, on it and years of extravagance followed as she decorated and lavishly furnished her 'home'. By 1704 it also contained the beginnings of a model court and town, her second absorbing interest, Mon Plaisir.

In 1715 the Princess converted to Roman Catholicism, to the further distress of her Protestant husband. He died the following year and his widow, with increasing money problems, continued to record in miniature her court, town and countryside; when his relations refused financial assistance she approached her new church and borrowed heavily from the Ursuline nuns. She still owed wages amounting to 3559 taler when she died in 1751, aged eighty-five, but she had created Mon Plaisir.

The plan of Arnstadt illustrated below was executed c. 1580. Although this was two centuries before Augusta Dorothea's recreation of the town, we can speculate that she followed the general layout and that various details, such as the chapel and formal gardens, derive from it.

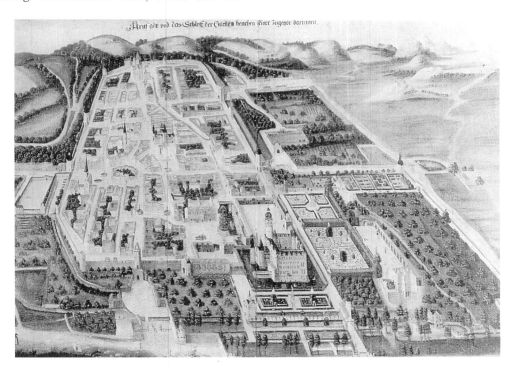

SALON WITH DECORATIVE WALLPAPER

The two pretty little rooms illustrated here and opposite are from a case of eight rooms, four upon four, which has been made to suggest a 'house'. These two are from the central part on the upper floor. The house itself stands on a base, also painted white, and is approximately nine feet wide by four feet high from the base-top to the balustrade. (In the centre of the balustraded flat roof there is another room, with a painted roof and a balcony upon which musicians are playing.) Both the ground floor salons have ruched silk curtains, and one has a fine corner fireplace with a painting inset into the overmantel. However, it is the upper pair which attract attention as their walls are decorated most elegantly and their occupants are delightful. In the room illustrated below they relax at home; their chairs, with delicate astragal legs and crimson velvet upholstery, and the inlaid cabinet against the wall are of much finer quality than the interesting tapestry frame and tea-table, with its silver teapot and eggshell porcelain teabowls.

Although an attempt has been made to suggest a finely decorated salon, it unfortunately draws attention to one regrettable omission throughout Mon Plaisir, the lack of carpets; though probably they were supplied as well as curtains originally.

SALON WITH MURAL

In the room next door to the one occupied by the relaxing trio a quartet of dolls create an entirely different ambiance; here they are obviously practising to perfect their performance later in the day.

These walls are beautifully decorated, although the hunting scenes depicted in the murals are not for the squeamish, and this is one of the few examples of a colourfully ornamented ceiling, the cupids being applied as a form of découpage.

The singer is charmingly attired in a shimmering dress of gauze over cloth of silver trimmed with lace; and the musicians are all in court dress, their fine crimson coats providing a colourful contrast to the off-duty gentleman in the adjoining room.

As will be seen also in Nostell's kitchen, the stand on which a figure is fixed is extremely irritating as it spoils the natural effect of the group; it is particularly annoying in this case as the head and hands of this musician are so realistic. Out of more than 400 dolls in Mon Plaisir he seems to be uniquely disadvantaged.

It appears the same person made the tables in both these rooms, though the most interesting pieces are the musical instruments with their intriguing difference in scale.

A HUNTING SCENE

This is one of the rare scenes in Mon Plaisir when an outdoor activity is depicted against a realistically painted backcloth.

Interest in this miniature replica of the court and town of Arnstadt invariably centres on the interiors, the living and work rooms, the shops and then the street-scenes.

There are, though, one or two beautifully painted sets of natural surroundings. The Albertin garden scene is one example; but it presents a formal, almost geometrically planned three-dimensional garden in the foreground, balanced by the symmetrical architectural structures painted on the backcloth.

This setting is anything but formal; a stag has been hunted across a wooded landscape and cornered in a grove of trees. Whilst all the ladies were placed in the court, embroidering or practising their music, these courtiers, to whom the chase was a serious if enjoyable sport, were portrayed in the surrounding countryside. The only formality is in their attire; although their coats are a camouflage green instead of their usual red, they are richly garbed and still wear their tricorne hats.

It is not a scene normally associated with Mon Plaisir, but the Princess Augusta Dorothea was a realist and saw that her project presented as many facets of daily living as possible.

A BED ALCOVE

Nobody knows for certain exactly how Mon Plaisir originally looked; but it does seem likely that the town's planner decreed that some buildings in the foreground should be on a larger scale than those at the back of the display. This was a perspective 'trick' often used to achieve a more realistic effect in large antique crèche scenes for example.

Since 1704 when the project was begun many changes have taken place; the miniature town has been dismantled and altered, many items broken and replaced, sometimes in different positions.

Possibly this 'room' was once a bed alcove of a larger chamber, a feature frequently found in important baby and miniature houses.

Now the magnificent effect of this ornately canopied and furbished bed is lessened by the over-large warming pan and night-cap in front and the equally out-of-scale gilt chair beside it.

Wherever they are placed, beds have to be made each morning and these two maid dolls appear to be enjoying a good gossip as they work.

Many settings in Mon Plaisir group into morning, afternoon and evening events as Princess Augusta Dorothea recorded 'a day' in her court and town. Some, like kitchens, are 'all day' sets, but this is surely a 'morning' room.

THE LYING-IN ROOM

The main walls in this interesting room are painted plain white, the necessary elegance being provided by the carved and gilded ornamentation of the columns, putti, the unusual pair of little circular mirrors over the window and the large framed mirror on the opposite wall, and the two paintings on the alcove wall.

The alcove itself is elaborately embellished. The central section has a richly patterned wallpaper (and almost the only carpet left in Mon Plaisir) and contains the ornate bed, which has crimson hangings and a suitably formal flower decoration at its head.

Such splendour provides a perfect foil for the plain ivory silk dress, trimmed with blue, worn by one of the Princess's attendants standing by the bed. Another well-dressed doll is in the blue moiré-lined right alcove.

The corresponding alcove on the left has a pretty pale pink and gold wallpaper, mostly hidden behind a screen adorned with Chinese figures, which is placed across this section.

In Mon Plaisir screens may hide more than the wallpaper for many rooms have doorways leading nowhere and seemingly inexplicably placed until one remembers Mon Plaisir's layout was far more realistic than the present arrangement, and what are now separate sections were previously connected.

DETAIL OF DOLLS

It was hardly to be expected that Princess Augusta Dorothea would omit from her replica one of the traditionally important rooms in any big house.

Like other German and Dutch collectors she created an imposing lying-in room – now in the 'house' featured on page 18. Framed by the alcove's arch a smiling nurse brings an elaborately swaddled royal baby to the mother; one cannot help wondering if the room is also a sad memorial to a baby who died, or perhaps the Princess's wishful thinking.

There is no record that she bore any children; but private papers prove that in those days sometimes still-born or very young infants' deaths were, officially, left unrecorded. Either way, the position of the mother's outstretched arms as she sits in this magnificent royal apartment is very poignant.

The condition of her brocade dress seems remarkably good if it is early eighteenth century. However, some of the dolls have been redressed, either under the aegis of Princess Marie von Schwarzburg-Sondershausen in the 1880s, or even as late as the 1930s when Arnstadt's Museum received the miniature town, and decided that experts should restore, where necessary, its 400 dolls and 2600 miniature objects before displaying Mon Plaisir.

A NURSERY IN A BURGHER'S HOUSE

As they are arranged at present all the rooms in the larger cases have to be viewed as entirely separate scenes; although groups may have been placed next to each other they were not chosen to represent a complete house with bedrooms, reception rooms and kitchen areas.

The nursery from a burgher's home, illustrated opposite and below, is next to one from a totally different household and they do make a most interesting contrast.

This young woman doll, wearing a fine lawn fichu and apron over a coral and green patterned dress, has been given at least daytime help with the children. Their security during the night has also been considered, for the lattice-work, box-like cabinet against the right wall is the older infant's safety cot into which a child could be shut at night and left, unattended but secure, until morning.

In this daytime scene the youngster occupies a special padded high-chair and is fortunate enough to have a tableful of toys.

The fashion for hanging pictures from bows has been revived many times since it was used in Mon Plaisir – perhaps the happy cherubs depicted are symbolic for a nursery; anyway, apt or not, they are rather appealing on the plain walls.

DETAIL – A CRADLE

Although the plain and simple chamber opposite is far removed from the splendour of the royal lying-in room, it too contains some fine examples of miniature woven canework. The hooded baby-linen container is smaller, but similar to the one in the palatial apartment.

This cradle is not so elaborate as the royal infant's as its only decoration is in the self-coloured woven pattern round the sides and the open weave of the curved hood, but it does have similar (undecorated) rockers and, like the scrap-decorated screen in the background, is a pretty and useful piece of furniture.

As the nurse and baby suggest, most of the Mon Plaisir dolls are supremely well made. Many of the courtiers' faces may have been portraits of living people; certainly they are, in the main, exceptionally full of character and the waxes have been carefully blended and moulded to suggest reality.

The Princess's confessors are usually credited with having made them, and it is probable that priests or artists skilled at making wax crèche figures would have been employed – one priest at the Augustenburg definitely made and signed a wax relief-portrait of the Princess in 1751.

A NURSERY WITH ORIENTAL WALL PANELS

A German booklet contains a reference to this room in Mon Plaisir and describes it as belonging to a civil servant's house. As the women occupants are very obviously related to the two babies, and are not employed as nursemaids to care for a German family's children, this does suggest that a male member of their family has a position at court.

African page-boys were often employed in large European houses during the eighteenth century and, as Princess Augusta Dorothea has such a character in one of her rooms, watching some courtiers playing cards, the fascinating group in this nursery could represent some of his relatives. The girl rocking a particularly well-modelled infant is dressed as a nursemaid, but the woman breast-feeding her baby is one of the most unusual in Mon Plaisir.

Although a Dutch house has a wet-nurse (page 141) nursing mothers are seldom seen in miniature houses and this finely dressed one is an unexpected and beautiful example. She certainly seems to be comfortably situated, judging by her silk brocade dress and the ribbon swaddling-bands round the baby.

The whole room, with Chinese panelled wallpapers, velvet padded furniture and brightly patterned curtains round the four-poster bed, is as delightful as the dolls.

A SALON WITH CERAMIC FIREPLACE

These subdued shades of the watered-silk covered walls (originally blue but now faded to green), upholstered velvet chairs, ruched curtains, and even one doll's dress, certainly provided a contrast to the room below. But this one also has a Chinese wall-scene though here a circular blue-and-white landscape is painted on the very unexpected glazed ceramic chimney-piece. It is the room's most remarkable feature and gives this cool-looking little apartment its own exotic touch.

There are other unusual items, the exuberantly carved silver-framed mirrors, pretty firescreen and musical instrument, but the very decorative chimney-piece is the dominant attraction.

More often than not the furniture in any scene at Mon Plaisir is a mixture of fine miniature pieces suitable for display and some attractive, but less well-made, examples; here, however, all the furniture is of matching quality, the chairs having particularly beautifully carved astragal legs.

In this elegantly decorated and furnished salon the two dolls at their tea-table could be representing court ladies relaxing away from their formal duties; but as the miniature Princess appears several times in Mon Plaisir, and usually wears a brocaded silk dress, quite possibly she is the figure on the left.

STREET SCENES

Strongly reminiscent of the old Rows of Chester, or the modern tiered Covent Garden complex in London, is this case with a balcony of booths above the shops – here not at street level but on the shelf below.

Looking through the glass front is sadly frustrating as it is a tantalizing reminder that Mon Plaisir was once laid out as a miniature town, with views up streets, down alleys and into shops and houses.

Midway along the upper shelf is a captivating little travelling theatre, with the famous harlequin doll, who is almost the logo of Mon Plaisir, attracting the attention of passers-by.

Those who know Germany's enticing *Christkindlmarkts,* the traditional open-air December markets sparkling with frost and decorations for Christmas, will recognize the adjoining booths as their design has not changed over the centuries.

The lower shelf has a real working-day atmosphere; two farmers, with a plough and a horse-drawn cart, apparently exchange greetings untempted by the shoe-maker's booth or the pottery seller's wares.

All these hundreds of tiny items are beautifully made and, as a record of life in early eighteenth-century Arnstadt, such a street scene is unique and invaluable.

A KITCHEN AND A WORKSHOP

Some smaller cases have painted roofs, although the settings they contain are a miscellaneous assortment of rooms and shops.

The end two in this example represent a kitchen situated above a completely unrelated cooper's workshop. Here cooking facilities are very primitive; under an enormous 'chimney' is an arched brick platform, upon which a cook is endeavouring to prepare food in various pots. A fire underneath the platform would heat the bricks, but it must have been an irksome task. (There is another even more elementary structure in the convent's kitchen, and both these simple rooms contrast starkly with the bustling, abundantly equipped palatial kitchen on page 36 and page 15 in colour.)

The coopers working in the room below clearly illustrate their craft; there are various casks and tubs on the floor and the two men are labouring to construct a large barrel. Although the workshop also contains two female dolls they are probably onlookers, or family, even though both are holding staves ready for the coopers to fix in position.

There are more staves on the table and hanging from the white-washed walls, and two shelves – directly below the well-stocked dresser in the kitchen above – display examples of their work.

Both settings are accurate miniatures and a fascinating record of people at work.

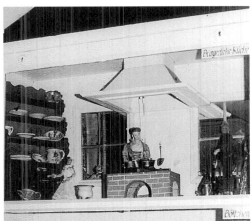

THE COURTIERS' SALON

An amusing touch in this otherwise sedate salon is provided by the occupants. The doll representing a wan-looking court lady trying to relax whilst wearing a tightly corseted dress and sitting on a stiff backed chair, is facing her opponent in a game of draughts set out on the table before them.

This slim young male doll is obviously a courtier off-duty as he wears a long robe instead of a formal coat and is about to exchange his wig for the cap in his hand so that he may relax in complete comfort.

It is an elegant, if small, room, with generously ruched curtains, a pair of mirrors in ornamentally carved and gilded frames, some good pieces of furniture and one of Mon Plaisir's rare paintings.

The walls are interesting as they have a scalloped gold border surmounting panels of crimson damask on a pale brown background reaching down to an unusual dado with inset decorative panels.

Both the lidded urn and stein are ceramic and may be from the faïence factory the Princess founded nearby, the Dorotheantaler-Fayence-Manufaktur; there are several small pieces, some marked with the maker's initials, still in the Princess's miniature court and town, although the factory was built to supply her own palace, the Augustenburg.

THE PRINCESS'S SALON

In this rather lovely room the only occupant who is relaxed is the dog; otherwise the atmosphere is extremely formal.

Blue seems to have been a favourite colour in rooms at the court of Mon Plaisir (although sadly now often faded to green). This one has a very decorative blue and silver wallpaper and geometric designed panels on the doors; there are also blue chair-covers and ruched curtains, and even blue and white porcelain ornaments.

As well as the dado (whose decoration matches the door) there is an elaborate chimney-piece, with a charming picture of roses hanging above the overmantel mirror.

The addition of another pair of picturesque silver-framed mirrors, a delightfully painted rather large firescreen and three inlaid or ornamental tables makes it a room fit for a princess – and one, Princess Augusta Dorothea, is using it as she partakes of a little light refreshment.

She is attended by a red-coated courtier and, as the other doll is wearing an identical coat to that worn by one thought to represent the Prince (see page 20) possibly this doll recalls her late husband in his younger days.

It has to be remembered that even a miniature Rome cannot be built in a day and the construction of Mon Plaisir took many decades, hence the 'ageing' of the two principal characters.

THE PALACE KITCHEN

This fascinating kitchen is the upper room in a two-storey building in Mon Plaisir.

As so often in miniature kitchens, many of the pots and pans are out of reach, for they hang from shelving above the decorative blue and white tiles covering the walls to the high mantel-shelf level. From there upwards to the ceiling the white walls support tiers of shelving, all filled with dishes and containers.

As imagination works overtime when viewing Mon Plaisir it is a relief to know that there is a long hook in this kitchen, customarily used to remove anything from such dizzy heights.

Although the cooking facilities are very basic the housekeeper, with a firm grip on her keys, and the two chefs preparing a good supply of food with their two busy kitchenmaids, are well supplied with implements. Additionally, even if all wood and water had to be fetched from outside, they do have a wall-mounted washbasin and towel. These pewter and wooden dishes are mostly for below-stairs use; the gold, silver and porcelain needed upstairs are kept in another room.

Imagining the smoke and fumes in such a kitchen it does seem a very odd position for the splendid painting framed above the fireplace, even if the scene is a domestic one.

Under the kitchen, in a lower part of the building (which has a basic façade) is the big wine-cellar. Through the central archway two aproned cellarers are hard at work with bottles, funnels and glasses testing the wine; a third is up on a stand examining a cask.

High above the kitchen, at roof-top level, a figure is emerging from the chimney (see the illustration below). Although other buildings have chimneys this is the only one being swept. The doll, dressed in a leather jacket and breeches with a soot-grimed head-scarf, probably represents a climbing boy with his brush rather than the master sweep. (There is another sweep in Mon Plaisir, but he is a curiously small figure half hidden by the enormous oven in the bakery.)

Many professions and trades in Arnstadt are demonstrated in Mon Plaisir. In the various buildings and room settings, from cellars to attics, dolls illustrate the way all stratas of society dressed, lived, worked – and existed in the case of the disabled beggar receiving dole from a nun at the convent door.

Street scenes also depict outdoor life; markets, complete with travelling players' booth as well as stalls, a mail coach halted outside a post office, street-vendors jostling farmers with horses and carts, it seems that everyone in Arnstadt is represented.

THE PORCELAIN ROOM

Both the Prince and Princess were keen collectors, although, probably of necessity because of her extravagance, he seems to have kept his interests under better control than his wife's mania for furnishing houses, big and small.

When, mainly because of debts incurred over the principality's upgrading, he was forced to sell his vast coin collection she continued to indulge her hobby and at the Augustenburg had a full-scale porcelain room as well as this scaled-down version in Mon Plaisir.

One of the fascinations at the extremely interesting Stadt Museum in Arnstadt is to look first at the breathtaking array of fine Chinese porcelain in a room whose walls are covered with exquisite examples on gold-and-white brackets, and the roped-off floor space has larger vases and figures on stands.

Moving directly to the baroque miniature porcelain room it is intriguing to see tiny versions on similar brackets and these circular stands on the floor.

The dolls supposedly represent the young Prince, in a yellow coat, giving a red-coated courtier a private view of the splendid display. Many of the minute pieces have contemporary markings (that is 1662–1722), and are Chinese export items, not, of course, ones from the Princess's own porcelain works.

A FORMAL SALON

This is the last scene in which the Princess appears, for the doll in widow's weeds traditionally represents her in later years. The room in which the group are sitting is one of the more realistic: the walls have a decorative dado with a suitably elegant silver-grey wallpaper above surmounted by an elaborately patterned frieze. The ubiquitous ruched silk curtains were a pretty shade of sea-blue, now faded, and they are fitted over realistic sash-windows.

Besides two or three pieces of good furniture there are a pair of matching gilt-framed mirrors and a fine painting, also gilt-framed, hangs over quite a detailed fireplace. The only thing out of scale in this attractive salon are the teabowls on the rather heavily-topped table, otherwise the room is charmingly harmonious.

There is one feature which catches the eyes not only of the beholders but, apparently, the seated dolls, who somehow manage to look delightfully at ease on stiff crimson upholstered chairs while their necks are craned as they, also, seem to be admiring the ceiling.

It certainly is very beautifully painted and it is amusing to see how appropriately natural this typical doll position is in these circumstances. Even more humorous is the way even the subject in the painting seems to be looking up at the pictorial ceiling-panel.

THE CONVENT

Throughout her marriage and long widowhood Princess Augusta Dorothea was beset with money worries. The mounting expense of furnishing Augustenburg (beside which Mon Plaisir's cost was a mere molehill) was an appalling drain on her husband's already extended exchequer, and her extravagant spending of money he himself needed for his own interests and collections caused endless arguments.

She converted to Roman Catholicism the year before he died and from 1716 the Princess frequently appealed not only to his relatives but to her new church for monetary assistance.

Her nearest source of succour was the convent at Erfurt, whose Ursuline order lent her considerable sums of money. The convent also provided many items for Mon Plaisir; not only did her confessors, installed in the Augustenburg, assist with the making of the wax dolls but the nuns immured in the convent itself made many of their costumes.

In this setting a group of nuns are depicted sitting at a well-supplied table in their refectory. One nun holds a missal and the customary reader of the religious book, to whom they listen as they eat, is already in the ornate pulpit – thus making it clear that their minds are on spiritual rather than material things.

THE CHAPEL

This realistic building, the chapel of Mon Plaisir, is an elaborately designed and ornamented structure.

It is unique in the whole complex of the court, town and country scenes for only this example remains of the original more natural-looking buildings. Several of the cases contain street-scenes which have painted backcloths with varying degrees of realism, and, except for the post house (which is the most elaborate structure with a painted street either side of the building), most of the three-dimensional shop fronts and 'houses' are very basic constructions.

The chapel is the sole building to be a complete miniature representation with very detailed decorations on the exterior walls, a double roof and a golden cross on top of the dome. Looking through the glass windows viewers can see the priests' habits are so detailed their orders are instantly recognizable (provided one knows what each order wears). The building's interior is also a meticulously realistic miniature replica, with a Mass being held in front of a full congregation. The altar is elaborate and made to look even more so by the curtains painted on the wall to either side; the columns are (painted) marble. The building also has an ornamented ceiling and some fine paintings; in fact, it seems a fitting tribute to the church of her adoption.

CHAPTER TWO

The Eighteenth-Century Dutch Cabinet House of Sara Ploos van Amstel

This superb example of a Dutch cabinet house is in the Gemeente-museem, The Hague. It is described, if that is the right word, as 'a cabinet of art curios with all those household articles appertaining to the same' in an inventory made after the owner's death in 1760.

The cabinet is large: six feet high by two and a half feet wide by two and a half feet deep, and Sara Ploos van Amstel paid the maker 230 guilders for it in 1745. Jan Meijjer was the craftsman who made it, and he played an important part in its conversion into one of Holland's finest 'hidden houses', as these cabinet houses are sometimes called. The nine rooms that had to be constructed or altered to fit into their new setting came from three other, earlier, 'doll cabinets' which Sara Ploos van Amstel had acquired some months previously.

The history of these 'doll cabinets' is both interesting and sad. The two lacquer ones, having five and six rooms, had been furnished some forty or more years before she bought them by the artist David van der Plaes, (who painted one of the pictures hanging in the 'collector's room').

After his death in 1704 'the widow Wijnershoff' had them in her possession; she also owned a larger, painted cabinet with eight rooms, which contained many items made by members of her family, well-known silversmiths.

It was these three late seventeenth- and early eighteenth-century little cabinets that Sara Ploos van Amstel gutted to create her far grander version; and it is almost impossibly difficult to be reconciled to their destruction, even when facing the wonderful results of such a tragedy.

Her splendid house consists of nine rooms, arranged on three floors. On the left of the cupboard's base is the lying-in room, on the right the kitchen, between is the courtyard/garden entrance. The grandest reception rooms are on the middle floor, with the music room on the left, the porcelain room on the right and a vestibule in the middle section. The top, attic floor contains, from the left, a 'collector's room', a linen drying room and a nursery.

It is fascinating to see how the miniature house mirrors real-life in so many ways; and not just by having small replicas of pieces of furniture and ornaments, or dolls dressed in perfect tiny versions of contemporary clothes.

In this cabinet house social history is illustrated in almost all its rooms: for example, the customary use of the lying-in room as a reception room and displaying there such status symbols as fine linen, or the use of a complete room to display a collection of porcelain; these arrangements make an immediate impact and reveal a lifestyle in a way no painting can equal.

While regretting Sara Ploos van Amstel's demolition of those earlier cabinets to construct her own contempory one, she must be blessed by all interested in the history of miniature houses for her meticulous record-keeping of every craftsman's name and every guilder she spent on the conversion and furnishing. Also for the accurate arrangement of the little replicas which give us such a fascinating glimpse into an eighteenth-century affluent Dutch home. Such an antique now, of course, interests not only dolls' house collectors but anyone intrigued by the past and how people lived centuries ago, and also those who just enjoy looking at beautiful things.

In Sara Ploos van Amstel's own time such a possession was displayed with pride. Her cabinet houses were placed in the reception rooms in her home; and it has to be remembered they would have been regarded not only as a cultured woman's hobby but as an acceptable status symbol – similar to the more usually seen porcelain room desired by so many Dutch and German collectors at that time.

SARA PLOOS VAN AMSTEL

Sara Ploos van Amstel, who owned this magnificent cabinet, had a rather impressive appearance herself, judging by this portrait. It was painted by the man who did so much work for her, Jurriaan Buttner, and now hangs beside her second cabinet house in the Frans Hals Museum in Haarlem.

Rarely is there such a well-illustrated link between owner, possessions and craftsmen for Sara Ploos van Amstel left her portrait, two cabinet houses and two notebooks of detailed records. Also recorded, in the archives of Amsterdam, are details of her birth and christening there in 1699 and her parents' name; she was the daughter of a banker called Rothe.

In 1721 she married Jacob Ploos van Amstel, a wealthy, cultured merchant, possessing a larger than average house in the Keizersgracht, the same street as the Rothes' family home.

Being childless she had more time and money to spend on her collecting. However, although she had at least one doll, with a trousseau, perhaps it was a childhood treasure, for her absorption with miniatures appears to have been, not compensatory, but a serious desire to acquire small replicas which recorded contemporary household styles. Her notebooks reveal such minute accounting one feels she must have enjoyed creating a 'hidden house'.

She died, tragically, in 1760 returning from her other home in Haarlem; the coach overturned and she was thrown into a canal.

HER SECOND CABINET HOUSE

Collecting miniatures for so many years meant Sara Ploos van Amstel had more than enough to assemble a second splendid, also fully-documented, cabinet house and it is interesting to compare the two. This second house has twelve rooms: looking always from left to right, in the basement are the kitchen, very well-equipped, a storeroom and an elegant dining room – with an adjoining lavatory. (That Sara Ploos van Amstel was first and foremost a recorder is emphasized as her own home's dining room, most unusually, was similarly situated.)

The main floor, above, contains a salon (later a dining room), with an alcove for miniature silver, not the usual porcelain, a centre vestibule, which is almost a twin to her first cabinet's and has an identical lantern and carpet, and the 'doctor's study'.

The next floor has the music-room, reception hall and the lying-in room. The attics contain a bedroom (originally a nursery), a linen drying room which is much bigger than the one in the first house, and another bedroom.

Sara Ploos van Amstel had interior doors, painted as a house façade, fixed behind the cabinet's black lacquer ones for additional realism.

This cabinet on legs has a most unusual feature – rachets to raise it and make viewing the basement easier. Her husband's niece inherited it but, in 1939, it was sold by her descendants; the Frans Hals Museum, Haarlem acquired it in 1958.

THE LYING-IN ROOM

Sara Ploos van Amstel followed a continental convention of her time by including a lying-in room in her miniature house.

In April 1743 she had bought at auction three old 'doll cabinets', acquiring them with a successful bid of 903 guilders. The lying-in room, originally in the third cabinet, was fitted into the beautiful walnut bureau to form the left hand room on the ground floor.

Such rooms were designed to reflect the family's status and taste – and to impress visitors calling to see the mother and new baby. The actual nursery was, as so often in real life, hidden away under the eaves, but the lying-in chamber was meant to be an elegant reception room.

This example, fifteen inches high, is elaborately and richly designed with a painted, scenic ceiling and bed alcove façade, embellished with gilded carving, and 'marble' pillars and fireplace.

The original, pre-auction, tooled-leather wall-coverings were replaced with pink moiré ones, probably to complement the splendid bed-canopy and coverings. Gilt-framed portraits look down upon the new baby's cradle and equipment, prominently arranged on the carpet. Somehow this display of costly antiques and new baby-linen is very endearing, and typically Dutch. The

detail below shows the occupants on the left-hand side of the lying-in room. They are worthy of attention as, like the chamber itself, they are a mixture of old and new workmanship. Sara Ploos van Amstel records in her invaluable notebook that she and Nigt Hoogehugse, her cousin, made the clothes for the doll wearing a blue dress and shoulder-cape. But the doll sitting by the fire-place in a pink dress with lace sleeves was attired by Jr Pastand and she, Sara records with satisfaction, 'has fine stones in her ears' and, it appears, a matching pearl necklace.

It is also recorded that these dolls had been given 'new heads and hands' before their re-dressing. Certainly their faces and hands are far more delicate than that of the highly-coloured doll holding the baby by the linen press in the picture opposite.

A scalloped length of pink silk, to match the bed-canopy, was also made by Sara and her sewing-woman, Johanna. It is fixed over the fireplace – a rather unusual addition to a 'marble' mantelpiece. The chairs have been upholstered to match the walls, and the final touches to this sumptuous room are provided by the exquisite, tiny blue-and-white 'porcelain' tea-set and vases, which are actually painted glass, and the silver items on the dressing-table.

THE ENTRANCE PORCH

If the lying-in room had windows there might have been a view of the middle section of the ground floor where Sara Ploos van Amstel and her designers created the illusion of an impressive entrance to a garden courtyard, with (painted) views beyond.

The porch, as it is described in the famous notebook, with its carved-out niches, is movable. It has been placed, at various times, at the back of the courtyard, framing the central view, and, as now, right in the front.

Before it was moved to its present position there were two 'marble' pedestals, supporting gilded statues, in front of the niches; these are now in the courtyard.

As the notebook records '. . . for the painting of the porch which is in the front of the cupboard . . .' it would seem the structure is now in its original position.

The painter, Jerriaan Buttner, of 'the porch . . . garden, views and perspective, and sky' received eighteen florins for these seven scenes, six of which were detailed perspective views.

Compared with the fee of twelve florins paid to Mijnheer ten Osselaar for painting the beamed ceiling of the kitchen and varnishing its tiles, it would seem that either one painter was grossly underpaid, or the other grossly overpaid.

THE KITCHEN

The ground floor's right-hand room is the kitchen. Again that third cabinet provided the setting, although, to fit it in to the new house, the height of the room had to be reduced a little and the beamed ceiling repainted.

It is perhaps an untypical room in several ways. Probably the most obvious reason for this is the difference in scale of both food and dolls, also furniture and accessories, permitted by Sara Ploos van Amstel. However, as she herself admits, she did 'place all sorts' of old and new items in the room, achieving a most attractive result even if the kitchen scales, so to speak, are a little unbalanced.

The large cupboards, with their painted decorative lower door panels, contrast vividly with the lower, smaller scale tables and chairs. The utensils hanging on the left-hand wall of the kitchen range from metal skimmers and pans, scoops and measures to salt-boxes and candle-sticks. The set of painted hanging shelves, almost excessively over-decorated, contains a beautiful, if over large, set of Japanese porcelain, obviously for use upstairs. Rather more accessible is the wooden rack containing eggs and the flagons on the cupboard-top below the shelves; and also the china colander and a footwarmer on the floor.

THE KITCHEN

Sara Ploos van Amstel seems to have been as interested in everyday kitchen and household linen as she was in her more valuable treasures upstairs. In this kitchen the shelf and mantel-shelf edgings are daintily scalloped, acknowledging a housewifely attention to detail below stairs as well as above.

Scale poses a problem over the platters of fruit on the table as the pears, for example, almost equal the size of the dolls' faces. All three dolls have wax heads and hands and are wearing pretty chintz dresses, mostly covered by their voluminous white aprons and more delicate lawn fichus. The 'housekeeper', standing just inside the door in this illustration, will be seen again, next time in the nursery (page 63).

Most Dutch miniature houses of this quality would have a elaborately equipped kitchen, perhaps with a storeroom for food, wine bottles and beer casks en suite. However, this attractive room is quite adequately supplied with copper and brass cooking pots and pans, milkcans and earthenware crocks, and there is a metal roasting spit attached to the fireplace.

The eye-catching set of three green painted metal containers decorated with a red design is particularly delightful and rather unusual.

THE COURTYARD/GARDEN

This section of the house was constructed by Jan Meijjer and then placed between the lying-in room and the kitchen. Its walls were painted with vistas down long formal garden-paths by Jurriaan Buttner, who seems to have made his name as a portrait painter before he came to Amsterdam in 1743 from Germany. Thanks to that invaluable notebook we know he also painted the courtyard's decorative pebbled area, for an additional fee of six florins.

If only he could have painted a portrait of those three cabinets before Sara Ploos van Amstel gutted them . . . from that tantalizing third cabinet she took the ornamental garden seats, now placed in front of the three painted vistas.

In the courtyard, open to the painted sky, are the inevitable blue-and-white ceramic objets d'art, a matching set of ten jardinières, two containing flowering plants.

The effect of the whole design depends on curves: on the trellis framing the vistas, on the elaborately painted and mirrored archways, angled each side of the central back view (which has its own curved steps), and in the striking marble parterre. This has as its centrepiece a most unusually shaped marble pedestal, surmounted by a little gilded cupid.

This section is almost a secret garden, half hidden behind the entrance-porch.

DETAILS FROM THE THE MUSIC ROOM

Before seeing the music room in its full splendour it is worthwhile having a closer look first at part of the left-hand wall of this well-appointed and artistically decorated reception room. Its visual attractions are obvious, but there are some aspects which could remain undiscovered without a 'guide book' footnote.

Sara Ploos van Amstel has recorded that the original owner of two of the 'doll cabinets' she bought was the artist, David van der Plaes; this room came from one of those cabinets and it seems he painted one of the landscapes decorating its walls – but which one? Tantalizing glimpses of these murals can be seen, when not obscured by furniture; this tranquil scene is next to the imposing chimney-breast. Like every other surface in the room the fireplace is painted; the mantelpiece simulates marble and the upper section wood, and a gilt-framed mirror hangs from the centre panel. Even the 'Turkey' carpet is painted – on fine canvas.

The silver miniatures, as is to be expected in a Dutch house, are very fine; two examples are seen here, the coffee-pot and little fitted cupboard. They may have been made by relatives of the second owner of those infuriatingly lost cabinets, Rachel Wijnershoff.

In the fireplace is a framed screen embroidered by Sara Ploos van Amstel; another one, almost identical, is placed in the 'nursery' and she made a third piece of needlework for the top of a hexagonal table in her second house.

The illustration on the right shows clearly the type of miniature items which the owner of the cabinet house thought the occupier might display in a case – his main (porcelain) collection was important enough to be given a separate room.

The minute chairs, sleigh and boxes are all Dutch silver, the little figures are carved ivory and there is just one fine piece of Dutch glass – the other examples have been put to good use in the room as wine goblets, rummers and decanters.

On top of the case are some good miniature porcelain pieces and on either side of it hang two of a beautiful set of six candle-sconces which caused Sara Ploos van Amstel to record she suspended 'from white silk cords silver sconces, of which four were in cabinet number two and the others I had made at a cost of 1.18 florins'.

It is difficult to distinguish the copies in this fine set, all hallmarked Haarlem silver.

MUSICAL INSTRUMENTS

In eighteenth-century Holland, music was deeply appreciated and musical instruments were to be found in most cultured Dutch homes. Indeed, Dutch paintings remind us that even in the more modest houses there would probably be at least a flute or mandolin.

Naturally Sara Ploos van Amstel included a music room in her plans for her new miniature house. 'In the room stands a clavier' she records in her invaluable notebook, 'it has been restored and repainted by Buttner, for which I paid him one florin. On the clavier music rest there is a music book, and in the drawer of a little table in the room are three similar books and two flutes. Also in that room is a viol da gamba'.

Both instruments came from the third of those old 'doll cabinets'; and again one wishes we knew what those early eighteenth-century cabinets looked like before Sara plundered them for her new house.

The decorative painting of the two instruments, though pleasing, is a trifle crude; and it is regrettable we cannot see the original painting of the clavier as its construction, with delicate twisted barley-sugar legs, suggests its first painting might have been more suitable in such a fine room.

THE MUSIC ROOM

Surrounded by so many lovely things, with decanters and glasses, a chess-board set with miniscule pieces and two tempting musical instruments, no wonder the two dolls look contented in their chairs.

On the right of the room the visitor, resplendent in a gold-braided coat and red silk waistcoat, retains his tricorne hat – though his gloves and fine dress-sword have been placed on a nearby chair. His host, comfortably relaxed in his splendid, if informal, red brocade robe, sits nearer the fireplace. The visitor, like the Princess and court ladies in their room in Mon Plaisir, leans back as if admiring the ceiling, as well he may for it is an interesting design and the panels of brightly coloured flowers are very attractive.

The indefatigable Sara Ploos van Amstel records she ordered these dolls especially: 'on two of these little chairs sit two dolls which I had made and with the clothing cost me three florins. These dolls were dressed as gentlemen by Meinheer Castang.'

The 'little chairs' she refers to were part of the set of 'six English chairs with red velvet seats' for which she paid the sum of 'thirteen guilders and ten stivers' though she does not note whether they were English style or English made.

THE VESTIBULE

It is very easy to overlook this vestibule, situated between two magnificent rooms on the first floor; but it is worth studying for its trompe l'oeil alone.

The walls, floor and ceiling appear to be grey-veined marble but are actually plasterwork painted by Jerriaan Buttner; Sara Ploos van Amstel records a twenty-five florin payment. The apparently moulded decoration over doors, archways and on the ceiling, suggests an elegant hallway to a no doubt equally splendid room beyond the centre door. By clever devices, a double archway, a flight of (painted) steps and three-dimensional door handles, a very satisfactory result is achieved, and a narrow, disproportionately high passage is transformed into an imposing vestibule. This use of trompe l'oeil and three-dimensional arches is most effective, both here and in Sara Ploos van Amstel's second house.

The vestibule contains only two items, excluding the carpet runner and rug. The gilded lantern is one of a pair, the other hangs in a very similar entrance hall in Sara Ploos van Amstel's other miniature house. The longcase clock, by Jan Meijjer, is visible only in profile here. The wax dolls only add to the vestibule's elegance – though the porcelain dog's position is decidedly questionable.

THE VESTIBULE CLOCK

This clock's face is, in fact, provided by a gold watch, otherwise hidden within the case. This is the watch/clock face about which some collectors love to argue. There is written evidence it was bought by Jacob Ploos van Amstel, but whether he gave it to his wife as a gift for her cabinet house or she appropriated it she does not relate in her famous notebook, so the point remains debatable.

The clock needs to be looked at from the front to fully appreciate all the work of its maker, Jan Meijjer; not only did he make the wooden casing but he also designed and made the metal ornamentation round the clock face, on the base section and, with a rather more delicate pattern, the edging on the centre door panel and for this work Jan Meijjer received four florins and sixteen stivers.

It was, of course, unnecessary for him to provide the winding chain, as Jacob's watch already had a gold chain attached to it; this, together with the pendulum, can be seen without opening the clock's door by peering through the little glass window, cut into the front panel and edged with gilt.

Although his wife did not explain how she came by the watch Jacob had bought, she does record that in the clock 'there is a small gold pocket watch with a gold chain, for which my husband paid Thr. Barrias the sum of twenty eight florins'.

THE PORCELAIN ROOM

It was the aim of most wealthy Dutch families at the time to have one room as a porcelain cabinet. Vast amounts were spent on exquisite pieces exported from China and a fine collection was an important status symbol.

Although Sara Ploos van Amstel's husband was a wealthy merchant he himself had no porcelain room, contenting himself with collecting sixty paintings, some drawings and a few medals. Sara, however, was an insatiable collector of miniature items and, if she had no full-scale porcelain room in her home it was no matter, she had a superb one in her dolls' house.

Jan Meijjer fitted this small porcelain room from the second cabinet into an elaborately decorated alcoved back wall for the grand new room. This is situated on the first floor which contains some of the finest rooms in the house. He designed eighteen gilded brackets to hold more pieces and fixed four large gilt-framed mirrors on the side walls, and two narrow ones in the alcove, to reflect the glorious display. The exuberance of the entire back wall is breathtaking; there are one hundred and twenty-five pieces of 'porcelain' – some actually painted glass – in the alcove alone.

In this illustration we can see how the table is covered with porcelain tea and coffee sets and the brackets support vases and figures. Only the tortoiseshell cabinet in the alcove is without porcelain, its four drawers being filled with minute shells.

There are many other treasures that are both lovely and interesting: the decorative painted ceiling, for example, reminiscent of many in large stately homes, and the charming chandelier, although perhaps too small for its splendid setting, rather casually suspended from the central panel. The carpet is of fine quality apparently but, in reality, painted on canvas; the time-consuming 'spot' technique was used to achieve the best effect. The beautiful set of English-style chairs, the tables with twisted legs, and the chinoiserie lacquer table and the little pedestal tables are also delightful. In any other room they would focus immediate attention, but even they cannot compete with such a wonderful display of porcelain.

It is interesting to compare the two early eighteenth-century miniature representations of 'porcelain cabinets' which are featured here in the Dutch cabinet house, and in the German Mon Plaisir on page 38. Both rooms have beautiful miniatures on gilded brackets fixed to every available wall space, and both designers have used mirrors to create the illusion of even greater splendour – a device frequently employed by collectors of regular-sized pieces.

Sara Ploos van Amstel's room perhaps has the more magnificent appearance because of its size and the beauty of its carpet and ceiling; Mon Plaisir now lacks both these assets. But, somehow, probably because in such a small, unfurnished space the eye is not distracted away from the porcelain in the room at Mon Plaisir, it more than holds its own with the larger Dutch version and its collection appears equally impressive, in quality if not quantity.

The colour chosen for the Dutch porcelain room's walls was not the usual white but a soft blue; a rather sophisticated choice as this shade does tend to blend the porcelain into the room's magnificence rather than make it stand out as its sole attraction.

THE CABINET

Even with closed doors as a piece of reception room furniture this walnut cabinet is impressive, with its fine inlay, ornate shape and ornamental pediment. Displayed this way it is admired as furniture while it keeps the equally magnificent treasure house hidden within, safe from prying eyes.

The top section of the cabinet merits special attention here, before looking at the layout of the attic floor of the house. The unusual shape of the pedimented top, which provides seven most artistic display brackets for the porcelain bowls, also affects the inner dimensions of the cabinet's upper rooms.

The conversion of this part of the cabinet presented several problems. Because of the contours of the piece itself, the rooms would have very oddly-shaped ceilings unless false ones were fitted. As the rooms were fairly low already great ingenuity was demanded to avoid this, especially in the 'collector's room' which needed height for a suitably proportional sanctum (see page 62). The chosen solution made a virtue of necessity and rooms were designed to fit the spaces using the cabinet's double curve as their ceilings; this is particularly effective in the collector's room.

THE MINIATURE CABINET

Few perhaps, unless very observant, would immediately realize this most practical piece of furniture in the lying-in room, the linen press, is an almost exact miniature replica of the grand display piece in which the house's nine rooms were reconstructed. Their basic design, although somewhat simplifed for the smaller version, is the same.

However, closer inspection reveals that the drawer handles and locks are larger in scale on the miniature; and there are only three, instead of the grander version's seven, blue-and-white 'porcelain' vases usually displayed on its pedimented top. Only five were in place when the photograph on page 42 was taken.

These linen presses were important pieces of furniture, and fine polished wooden doors hide an impressive amount of linen, bed-covers and blankets. Brides-to-be and housewives with a satisfactory display to show to friends, could, by merely leaving open a cupboard door, as has been done in the lying-in room (page 46), illustrate their enviable status in an acceptable and conventional manner.

THE COLLECTOR'S ROOM

The two most impressive pieces of furniture are placed side by side in this odd little 'collector's room'; the second, which is against the left wall, is inlaid with palmwood and has ebony feet, and it holds a collection of tiny shells, embedded in wax for extra protection.

Between the paintings of cattle on the back wall, placed under the dipping ceiling section, is a large walnut bookcase. This is filled with 'real' books bound in red leather, Biblical prints and parts of the *Odyssey* – in eighteen tiny volumes. Another book lies conveniently near the daybed, which looks most comfortable with a 'Hungarian flame' patterned cushion and cover. Yet another volume has been placed on the second of a pair of fine presses along the right wall; the first one has a beautiful filigree silver casket on its well-polished top. A mirror in a carved gilt frame hangs between these two pieces of furniture against an exeptionally pretty wallpaper, with dull gold background and bright swags of flowers looped up with coral coloured bows.

This is a strange and attractive little room to find so unexpectedly in an attic.

THE NURSERY

Although better suited to an attic than the left-hand room this nursery, in the top right section of the cabinet, is also an odd room, especially for a child. This poor little wax doll, with an attractive cap and long dress, carries a toy; but the curious little blue padded chair is the only nursery item to be seen.

The ceiling, shaped like the one in the collector's room, is blue and the floor apparently stone or marble; only its plain white walls seem suitable to the room's position. The fireplace is elaborate for an attic; the marble mantelpiece has a blue fabric edging partly obscuring the attractive tiled grate, and surmounting it is a carved-wood chimney-breast with a delightful painted scroll-edged panel.

The elegant four-poster bed, with a decoratively edged pale yellow brocade canopy and curtains, would grace any lady's chamber and suggests the room was adapted for nursery use.

It seems a comfortless nursery, without even a warm rug on the cold-looking floor. And where is the nursemaid? The 'housekeeper' seems to be baby-minding – or was nurse just visiting the kitchen? (See page 49) Certainly the doll's 'keys', which would be the housekeeper's insignia, look more like nurse's scissors.

THE LINEN DRYING ROOM

The middle section of the attic, it is almost a relief to see, is completely mundane with plain white walls and pale grey woodwork: it is a typical attic linen drying room.

Sensibly, to make full use of circulating air, the back wall is slatted and, below the (lowered) ceiling there is a wooden rack for drying and hanging clothes. Both features are found in most continental houses, full-scale and small, as a linen drying room was a basic essential in a town house without a garden.

This one is abundantly well equipped, with a good assortment of linen baskets hanging on the wall and scattered over the wooden floor. These baskets, here filled with clothes and linen, are attractive miniatures in themselves as their workmanship is very fine; considering their fragility, their splendid condition is remarkable.

The trestle-table holds a more unusual example of canework; in order to keep the nightcap's shape it has been fitted over a cane cone to dry.

The Dutch housewife's acknowledged expertise and pride in her home is well displayed in this simplest of little rooms. However, fitting it into the cabinet was less simple; its size meant two unsightly gaps occur between its side walls and those of the neighbouring rooms.

A LINEN PRESS

In this linen drying room, against the far left-hand wall, is a piece of furniture which, at first glance, looks like a book-binding press; however, its function is purely domestic as it pressed smooth the household's linen.

This actual press stands on a cupboard, which would contain linen not considered fine enough to keep ready for display – in the lying-in room for example.

Although it probably smoothed sheets more quickly and just as effectively as an iron (which in those days needed to be reheated frequently), using the press could have been an equally tiring chore. The heavy central screw, adjusting the pressure on the wooden boards, looks as if twisting it up and down would be hard work for a young laundry-maid.

These presses were part of the normal furniture in every big household and collectors usually took care to include one in their miniature houses. Sara Ploos van Amstel placed another in her second house's larger linen drying room; and two more interesting examples can be seen in Petronella de la Court's house in the Centraalmuseum in Utrecht and in the Gontard cabinet house in the Historisches Museum, Frankfurt. Here, as this otherwise very fine house has no linen drying room, the press was considered important enough to be placed on the landing.

CHAPTER THREE

The Twentieth-Century American Fairy Castle of Colleen Moore

This fairy-tale Castle, designed as a palatial home for fairies invisible to human eyes, took the mere mortals involved nearly a decade to design, construct and furnish.

Its dimensions are large as it is nine feet square, with the main tower rising to a height of twelve feet; its scale is one inch to the foot, in time-honoured measurements, or one-twelfth human size.

Hidden under the specially made platform on which the Castle rests, are all the mechanical devices necessary for its electric lighting and its plumbing, as both bathrooms, kitchen and fountains are well supplied with running water.

Two hundred separate pieces of aluminium were needed for its construction this material being chosen for its durablity and suitability for moulding certain sections.

The four men responsible for the making of the Castle must be mentioned. Charles Morrison, the father of Colleen Moore for whom the Castle was made, was helped by Jerry Rouleau, a fine technician, and two Hollywood set designers. Horace Jackson, who created the Castle itself to be 'an illustration in a fairy tale', and Harold Grieve, who was its interior decorator.

Obviously, as seven hundred artists and craftsmen were to be involved during the nine years it took from 1926 to complete this unusually decorated palace, they cannot all be listed. Between them they created detailed murals, floors and panels of painted ivory, rose quartz, jade and many other precious materials. They etched glass for windows and designed trees with waving branches and fountains, which flowed, for the garden and hundreds of miniature items for the Castle itself. Perhaps the most famous of these is the golden chandelier in the drawing room, which was made by H. Crouch, a jeweller, who used many diamonds, emeralds and pearls from Colleen Moore's own jewellery to create this exquisite, working miniature masterpiece. Or perhaps the choice should be the quarter-inch slippers for Cinderella or . . . but how can anybody choose one from so many wonderful things?

All its eleven rooms have a fairy-tale theme. The great hall has the Brothers Grimm's and Hans Christian Andersen's immortal stories illustrating the domed ceilings; while its wall-paintings feature Alice, Snow White, and even modern favourites like Mickey and Minnie Mouse.

The drawing room highlights Cinderella, whilst tapestries in the medieval dining room are based on Arthurian legends. The kitchen en suite, plentifully supplied with silver, glass, Sèvres and Royal Doulton porcelain, Delft pottery and pewter is, like the wine store above, decorated with *Mother Goose* murals.

The Prince's bedroom has many oriental pieces of furniture, but its theme is a Russian fairy story. Its adjoining bathroom, fit for Neptune himself, has a bath and ornamental shells of alabaster – the lavatory is gold.

The Princess's bedroom is exquisitely delicate and her bathroom is made of crystal and jade.

Ivory and gold are the chief materials for the chapel's carvings, altar and organ. Fine stained-glass windows have Biblical scenes, and precious stones adorn both vigil light and icon. Its ceiling is a miniature *Book of Kells*, whilst its floor is a mosaic inlaid with Biblical symbols.

Once a collector, always a collector; although the Castle was completed in 1935 one of the chapel's treasures is a tiny glass screen made from a fragment rescued from a 1940s blitzed window in London's Lambeth Palace.

The final room, with views across Aladdin's garden, is the shimmering blue library, where our tour of this fabulous Castle ends. However, between the chapel and the library is a passage, decorated with an amusing Noah's Ark mural.

Above this is the Castle's official treasure room. Remembering the many treasures on view throughout the Castle one wonders who chose the items regarded as so special as to be placed in hidden security – and however was the choice made?

COLLEEN MOORE

Kathleen Morrison was two when her father, to their mutual delight, made the first of her six dolls' houses, a simple plaything. However, the contents of her fourth house included many minute treasures of silver and porcelain, mostly relatives' gifts to an appreciative little girl.

By 1926, Kathleen Morrison had become Colleen Moore, the famous film star. She lived Hollywood style, and the 'fantasy factory' influenced the design of her seventh amazing house, the fairy-tale Castle of childhood daydreams when her imagination transformed sunlit clouds into fantastic palaces.

During the time that this dream was turning into reality she and Harold Grieve, the Castle's interior designer, frequently travelled abroad to find many of its antique treasures.

Finally in 1935, it went on public view, beginning many years of fund-raising for charity. In 1949 Colleen Moore lent the Castle to Chicago's Museum of Science and Industry, finally giving it to them in 1976. However, to the end of her life, in 1988, she maintained an active interest in her much loved treasure.

It is an entirely fitting touch of fantasy that, although she made many films, only here can we hear the voice of this star of silent movies, for Colleen Moore herself recorded the commentary which guides visitors round her enchanting Castle.

REGALIA TABLE AND CINDERELLA'S SLIPPERS

It is difficult to believe in the existence of two of these miniature items, which were specially placed in front of the regalia table for the photograph to highlight both treasures. In a fairy-tale castle one might expect to find Cinderella's slippers; to discover that these tiny shoes are only just over a quarter of an inch long, transparent and hollowed out so that they could be worn, almost makes one believe in fairies as it is so hard to realize that human-sized hands made them.

Colleen Moore was adamant they should not be solid, even travelling to Italy hoping a Venetian glass-blower could make the shoes she required; all told her it was an impossible task. However, back in America, she discovered a retired Michigan glass-blower named Rohl who created this pair of fragile, high-heeled shoes trimmed with crimson glass bows.

Behind Cinderella's slippers, and the gold jewel casket, the regalia for the Castle's 'owners' rests on a silver table. Like his sceptre and orb, the Prince's crown is gold, encrusted with rubies and sapphires. Pearls, diamonds and a minute emerald shamrock adorn the Princess's more delicate golden crown and wand.

The intricate rose/vine border of the great hall's ivory floor may also be clearly seen in this illustration.

THE GREAT CENTRAL HALL

That this Castle, though miniature, is magnificent is immediately made evident by the great central hall. It has an interior 'frame' of golden pillars reaching up to a deeply pointed arched frieze, decorated with another rose/vine motive and figures sculpted in high-relief, which both contrasts with and complements the exterior setting.

Outside, the Castle's silvery walls and turrets, with elaborately moulded decoration rising to the crenellated parapet, appear to be almost iridescent. Inside, the mellow golden colour of the great hall is designed to radiate a welcoming glow, as well as to display most effectively some valuable little objets d'art.

Illustrations, from Andersen's and the Brothers Grimm's stories, decorate the many-facetted ceiling domes; and the elaborately carved centre archway is surmounted by a sculpted panel depicting the Pied Piper at work.

Characters from fairy stories: Jack and the Beanstalk, the Princess and Seven Swans and Prince Charming have been etched on the glass panels of the tall, curved windows which touch the ceiling of the two-storey high great hall.

In front of the windows there is an eye-catching curved 'flying' stairway, which would surely induce vertigo if the building had human inhabitants, but is entirely suitable for a fairy-tale castle.

When referring to the Castle the term 'Hollywood Disney' has sometimes been applied in a rather disparaging way – usually by those who have not actually seen it. That two of its creators were Hollywood designers is undeniable; but their inspiration seems to have been pure vintage Hollywood at its magical best, and any Disney-like touches would relate more to Fantasia than any typical cartoon. (However, one watercolour picture of Mickey and Minnie Mouse is included among the paintings, as stars representing 'movies that are modern fairy tales'.)

From a more traditional story is the little sculpted Goose, with tiny golden eggs, on a gold and enamel table in the great hall.

The exquisitely carved ivory statue, of the mythological Pluto and Persephone, is an eye-catching example of the miniature objets d'art Colleen Moore loved to collect; two more ivory items are the filigree cabinets, one containing miniscule bottles and the other ivory carvings, along the right-hand wall.

As this is a film star's castle the two knights in shining armour, guarding the central entrance to the garden, are particularly apposite; not only are they most suitable for their setting but they once belonged to another famous star of the silent movies, Rudolph Valentino.

The great hall contains an extraordinary mixture of ancient and modern miniatures; some of considerable value, like the tiny figurines from a tomb in ancient Egypt, and some unique modern items, such as the miniscule glass slippers and the paintings of Colleen Moore's famous friends in storybook roles.

To create a setting which would be suitable both for rare museum pieces and a small painting of the King and Queen of Hearts as portrayed by Mickey and Minnie Mouse is no mean feat; but the designer of the Castle's hall was inspired to produce an entrance which is such an amazing blend of architectural splendour and fantasy that both these component parts can be accepted as entirely relevant.

Because Harold Grieve, the Castle's interior decorator, was a Hollywood set designer working for a famous film star, Colleen Moore, it seemed a natural progression to include cartoon characters with time-honoured storybook personae in decorations for her fairy-tale Castle for, as one of the illustrators pointed out, such films are the only 'fairy stories' some modern children know.

Colleen Moore was once described by a film critic as a 'grown up Alice' and, in this realization of her childhood dream she fully approved and expected such touches in her wonderland Castle.

TREASURES AND PORTRAITS

It is hardly surprising that even in a fairy castle it was thought necessary to protect, with red ropes fastened to bronze pillars, the statues under the paintings between the flight of steps on the left and the staircase in the great hall.

These statues, some of the oldest antique miniatures collected by Colleen Moore, were found in Egyptian tombs. So also was the alabaster jar, for kohl originally, on one of the pillars nearer the silver regalia table; the second pillar holds a Thai porcelain urn, believed to be over a thousand years old.

Interesting though these lovely items are, most eyes will wander to the paintings above the statues, and to the left of the arch. The left-hand groups of three, just visible in the illustration on page 72, are of Alice, actress Marguerite Clark posing as Snow White, and Miss Muffet by Willy Pogany.

All the paintings were either posed or painted by Colleen Moore's friends, and the two most interesting ones hang above the statues. Nearest to them on this wall is a portrait of Judy, her daughter, as Fairy Princess, painted by Frank Lackner, and the topmost one is of Colleen Moore herself in her screen role as Irene; perhaps her most famous portrait, is by Leon Gordon.

DRAWING ROOM MURAL

In this illustration we are able to see clearly the quality of the murals in the drawing room. Their theme is Cinderella's story and this panel depicts her entering the golden coach to go to the ball, waved on by her fairy godmother. They were painted by George Townsend Cole, who was also responsible for the ceiling.

All these panels, like the archways, have delicately carved 'frames'. However, the most intricate carvings in the room are on the columns decorating the staircase's entrance archway. Like the murals' edgings, these tiny carved figures have been painted in soft colours, and represent characters from German fairy stories.

Two more pieces of silver furniture are highlighted: a finely worked high-backed settee and an exquisite secrètaire with inset painted enamel panels. Standing on this lovely piece is a tiny ivory statue of William Tell.

On the steps several pots of flowers have been arranged and, just as casually placed, by the centre archway is an amber vase; five hundred years ago it was owned by a Chinese Dowager Empress. This deliberate blending of valuable antique miniatures, of interest to adult collectors, and a story-book decor, designed to appeal to children, is used very effectively throughout the Castle.

THE DRAWING ROOM

As with many rooms in the Castle, the drawing room's exterior silvery-blue 'frame' accentuates the effectiveness of the colour-scheme within. With a floor of rose quartz bordered with jade, which craftsmen working in China took nine months to make, the sparkling chandelier and the silver furniture, the whole room appears to shimmer with light.

The room's interior design is interesting. Between its front and back high curved arches the domed centre ceiling, painted to resemble a cloud-scattered sky, fans out to meet the many-curved chimney-breast, the curved arches of the staircase and those over the centre and side doorways.

The staircase, in the corner opposite the fireplace, leads up to the first floor; like most of the room's plain surfaces, its arched entrance has some intricately carved decoration.

The walls have the most detailed murals in the Castle and the chandelier, of course, is the most delicate of all the designs.

Apart from the gold longcase and gem-studded mantelshelf clocks there is only one piece of furniture that is not silver – the piano which is made of inlaid rosewood and has ivory legs.

The music manuscripts by the piano were hand-written by the composers, at Colleen Moore's request, and included works by Rachmaninoff, Stravinsky, Irving Berlin and Richard Rogers.

For quieter moments, one of the world's smallest ivory chess sets is placed on a nearby table.

SILVER FURNITURE

Usually, if silver furniture is placed in an otherwise realistic miniature house, though the items themselves may be beautiful and valuable, they look out of place.

One of the chief delights about the Castle is that such pieces are entirely acceptable.

In this room there are some lovely examples of the silversmith's work. Some, like these chairs and footstool, have been 'upholstered' with very fine needlework. The colours chosen for the silks were pale blues (now faded to green), echoing the shades in the murals, with delicately embroidered flowers of soft pinks and blue. This colour-scheme not only tones in with the wall-paintings, it enhances the effect of the shining silver.

The chair on the left has an unusual circular back with an open design of angels and cherubs and twisted 'rope' legs and stretchers ... incidentally, one wonders if the front stretcher design is, accidentally, an elaborate 'M' for Moore.

The armchair is more conventional – though that word is hardly fitting – since its chief beauty is its delicately patterned chasing.

The silver table is a blend of similar chasing and fine modelling; the face-masks on which the top rests have amazing detail and the legs are very elaborately designed.

In the scroll-edged silver frame on the table is the smallest portrait of Colleen Moore as a young girl.

DETAILS FROM THE PRINCESS'S BEDROOM

The Princess's bedroom, featured on page 78, is furnished with so many beautifully made miniatures that it is a pity all of them cannot be seen in detail. The examples in these two illustrations were chosen to represent some of the finest and also two of the most famous and valuable pieces in the Castle.

What must be one of the world's smallest sets of toilet items was made for this room. The golden mirror, comb, nailfile and hairbrush – this is diamond studded and all of three-quarters of an inch long – are placed on the dressing-table. This ivory piece also holds tiny matching gold boxes, in one of which lies the Princess's engagement ring, a diamond one, of course. It is amazing to see these miniscule miniatures and realize they were made by even the most skilled mortal jeweller; that Guglielmo Cini, a Bostonian, created a diamond ring of that diminutive size is almost incredible.

In the illustration opposite it is possible to see the toilet-set and boxes, and to appreciate the delicate tracery of the filigree door panels of the dressing-table itself. The pair of tables, one each side of the piece, are made of ivory too and hold one of the many lovely little bowls of flowers in the room; they also support a fan and, of all things, a telephone. The golden-framed looking-glass hanging on the wall between is ornamented with carved and gilded cherubs and flowers.

In front of the dressing-table is one chair from a set of beautiful Battersea enamel pieces of furniture; Colleen Moore searched for years to find matching chairs and settee.

In the illustration on page 78 of the whole bedroom, and also worthy to be seen in detail, are some of the Princess's musical instruments, particularly the lute and her gold and ivory harp placed near the left window.

All the room's ivory pieces are entirely delightful; the furniture, spinning-wheel and bird-cage are exquisitely made.

The best known miniatures in this room are the two jewelled silver chairs, either side of the ivory table. Their green enamel 'cushions' match the emeralds which, with diamonds, were used to make the dress-clips from which the chair backs were fashioned. Although the jeweller's skill is undeniable it is perhaps regrettable that Colleen Moore allowed her jewellery to be adapted for the purpose as the original dress-clip design does seem a little obvious.

THE PRINCESS'S BEDROOM

This is a most charming and dainty bedchamber, entirely fit for a fairy princess. Although this is one of the few rooms without a fairy-tale theme, it does have wall decorations and items of furniture with fairy-tale connections. The colour scheme is delicate, mainly warm ivory tones with, inevitably, touches of pale gold; the floor provides the shimmering effect as it is made of mother-of-pearl sections with an inlaid gold border pattern.

Two of the ivory-coloured walls have very realistically painted insects and little winged fairy creatures, many playing musical instruments, others resting on leaves and cobwebs; these decorations adorn the windows and right-hand walls.

Gold painted scroll-work ornaments the cornice, and the ceiling's centre panel is reminiscent of Italian frescoes.

As the long, rather gothic windows of differing size have fragile frets encasing the pale amber stained-glass insets of birds and flowers, it is, perhaps, just as well additional lighting comes from two golden candle-chandeliers, hanging each side of the painted ceiling panel.

On a gold-rimmed dais rests the golden shell-shaped bed carved with crowns, shells and cherubs, two of which hold back ivory silk curtains descending from a small circular canopy ring, surmounted by another crown. (Legend has it that the Sleeping Beauty was this bed's first owner.)

THE PRINCESS'S BATHROOM

Both the Princess's bedroom and the Prince's across the hallway have adjoining bathrooms. His bedroom contains some fine oriental pieces, although its theme is a Russian fairy story; however, although undoubtedly fit for a Prince, it does seem to lack the charm of her room.

His bathroom is very ornate, with an alabaster bath and a gold lavatory, but, again it does not perhaps equal the beauty of hers. Her bathroom presents an astonishing blend of fantasy and practical fact as imagination is combined with a knowledge of plumbing. It is very beautiful; the pale jade and crystal used to construct it provide softly glowing surfaces, against which silver pieces sparkle and shine.

Appropriately, the theme is the legend of the water-sprite, Undine; her story is etched on to the walls, and her statue on a plinth of precious stone, in the central alcove, provides the one warm touch of colour in this shining 'grotto'.

The crystal ceiling, etched with birds and butterflies, is supported by crystal columns.

Like the tulip-shaped wash-stand, the filigree cabinet, settees and table, the bath itself is silver. It resembles a fountain base, the bathwater coming from the mouths of silver sea-creatures decorating it, while their tails support tiny cupids, and swans adorn the bath's rim.

LIBRARY CONTENTS

The furniture for the library was specially designed, and almost every piece has a surprisingly original, not to say extraordinary, shape. As the room has a mainly marine theme it was fairly predictable that the designer would incorporate shell shapes into his furniture patterns; far less predictable was his choice of rotund little cockle shells as 'legs' to support the sofas, fire-side stool and one table top. The group of scallop-shell chairs, even the chess table and lectern with slim sea-horses for 'legs', look positively conventional by comparison.

All the shells appear to be made of sea-soaked bronze – the resulting verdigris most suitably linking them to the room's colour scheme.

The bookcases are also made of 'bronze'; again seahorses have been used as supports, this time they hold up the curiously shaped top-sections, which are 'folded back' from each central arch to reveal their star decoration. Some of the shelves have been used to display a small but beautiful collection of ivory figures and animals. At least two-thirds of the books were specially made for this library and are not only finely-bound miniature volumes, with covers of gold-leaf decorated kid leather, they are also unique.

Colleen Moore commissioned these tiny books (their average size is one inch square), and asked the makers to bind blank pages. These were then sent to a selection of famous modern writers with the request that they should copy something from their published works on to the paper. A surprising number of authors agreed and the library boasts hand-written volumes by such diverse writers as Conan Doyle, F. Scott Fitzgerald, John Steinbeck, James Hilton and Eleanor Glyn. Placed in a prominent position on the library table there is even a copy of *The Enchanted Castle*, written by Colleen Moore herself; all this section of the library therefore contains not only first, but also only editions.

Two diminutive modern albums hold minute photographs of film stars and European royalty and another album is filled with autographs of 'persons who have contributed to Twentieth Century Progress'. It holds a fascinating assortment of signatures: Queen Elizabeth II and Winston Churchill, the Duke and Duchess of Windsor, The Emperor of Japan and General Eisenhower, Pandit Nehru, Franklin Roosevelt, Charles de Gaulle, Toscanini and Henry Ford, to name but a few.

Illustrious authors from the past have not been forgotten and one bookcase holds miniature volumes printed between 1820 and 1900.

Architecturally the library is appropriately grand for a castle; and the interior decor, which soars up to the solar system on the domed ceiling from the zodiac signs inlaid in the floor, includes both painted ships and three-dimensional mariners and is somewhat breathtaking.

But in a fairy castle nothing need be taken too seriously and surely only the most disgruntled of mortals could fail to be amused, if not fascinated, by the inspired exuberance of the library furniture.

There is a pleasing anecdote about the designer who became so exasperated by the solemn attitude of a reporter who asked him what period he would call the furniture's style, that he replied shortly 'early fairy'.

The combination of these surreal pieces and the realistic portrayal of human characters in the murals and frieze framing this room is rather reminiscent of the artist Salvador Dali's dual qualifications – though perhaps Lewis Carroll also come to mind.

It is all too easy, in this most imaginative room, to let one's own imagination run riot and to picture an inhabitant of the Castle sitting in a shell-chair, glancing through the doorway at Cinderella's coach outside and then picking up the miniature volume of the works of F. Scott Fitzgerald.

THE LIBRARY

As the rooms' 'frames' link in with their themes this one may seem unrelated at first glance, apart from its toning colours. However, it illustrates one of the famous story books, *The Adventures of Robin Hood*.

Just visible behind the central outer arch is the ceiling dome, made of copper and painted to depict the constellations; and the library floor, of rare woods, is inlaid with signs of the zodiac.

The room's main theme is marine, so sea and sky are linked by the wall-paintings, the carved figures of famous fictional mariners, Gulliver, Robinson Crusoe and Captain Kidd over the two doorways and the fireplace and the library's stellar decorations.

Another kind of star appears in the fireplace mural; Neptune's face is a portrait of the film star Wallace Beery. The massive fireplace decoration reaches high up the wall. Fishing nets, of perforated metal, form the ornamental swags which surround the grate and Neptune's mural, and are gathered beneath the carving featuring Captain Kidd.

Appropriately, the andirons and bronze anchors and capstans, of bronze also, support burning logs in the firebasket.

Aladdin's Garden may just be visible through the two archways, one either side of the fireplace.

Incidentally, the steps and the bookcases' platforms are not wood but tortoise, or in this room is it turtle shell?

THE STRONGROOM

In every castle one would expect to find a strongroom for the safe keeping of its special treasures. It really does take quite a search to find such a room in this Castle and, when finally discovered, the puzzle is to work out how such a room could be entered.

If we remember, fairy-tale treasure is usually found at the foot of the rainbow; with this clue it is possible to find one place in the Castle where the strongroom might be – behind a mural illustrating an amusing scene, entitled 'Love in Bloom', depicting a line of pairs of amorous animals leaving the Ark. It is painted along the wall of a narrow passage, and in it is a concealed trap-door. The only way into, and, with more difficulty, out of the strongroom is to open the trap-door and let down a rope into the strongroom below.

Even then a metal grid separates any potential thief from the treasure and, in the dim light, the strongly realistic painting of Ali Baba on the back wall might well seem to be a real guardian.

Between Ali Baba and the bars lies a vast trove of miniature valuables: gold, silver and porcelain objets d'art lie uncovered on the floor and chests hide still more treasures. To quote from the inventory 'these vary from precious miniatures to antique charms, souvenirs of famous fairyland parties'. There are also bejewelled flagons of love potions, wizard cloaks of invisibility, rings of enchantment and power and magic wands.

CORNER VIEW OF THE CASTLE

The first illustration of Colleen Moore's Castle shows only its impressive entrance side, with the great hall's high windows clearly visible. This final view shows more of the Castle's construction as the camera has been angled to show the right-hand side wall also. From the front to the towers at the far right-hand corner it is covered by a glass panel to provide a clear view of the interior, while protecting the contents from damage and dust. Both back and left-hand walls have similar glazed sections, so only from the front can the Castle's exterior architectural splendour be properly appreciated.

The balcony, overlooking the garden, is ornamented with painted panels illustrating Don Quixote riding with Sancho Panza and tilting at windmills. All the paintings, in separate medallions on the nearer, right section, are of characters from *Aesop's Fables*, with the Stork, Fox and grapes placed on the central arch of the library's roofed terrace.

The carvings over the entrance and the three rondels on the library roof all depict fairy-tale characters, birds, beasts and goblins; the bigger panel, on the chapel's garden wall, features a Wizard of Oz scene to carry the fairy-tales right up to the twentieth century.

As the Castle is wired for electricity all the lamps outside, like the fixtures within, are lit. Above it a ceiling over the viewing area depicts a cloudy sky. Real clouds, the inspiration for the Castle, were sunlit; this dream-castle-in-reality, so to speak, glistens under a sky painted with a smiling sun/moon for this time-warp Christmas Eve.

Even fairy-tale castles need water, for ornamental if not practical purposes. In the centre of the walled garden is a weeping willow; and not only in name, for this amazing example actually drips minute 'tears' of real water from its branches. To the right of this lachrymose specimen is another tree, also perpetually active; this time its boughs, as yet unbroken, have to rock the nursery-rhyme cradle – which is clearly seen in the photograph of Colleen Moore on page 68. So much magic is illusion, unfortunately, but all, except perhaps the youngest visitors to the Castle, probably wonder how they work.

As well as the pipes and wires, unseen under the blue curtains draping the stand, is a piece of machinery as fascinating in its own way as any item on display. For over fifty years it worked continuously to keep the willow and its neighbouring tree weeping and waving. Inevitably one part wore out; however, the firm who originally made the mechanism were still working, and were able and delighted to replace it. The veteran, it is pleasing to report, is now resting in the firm's museum.

To receive the guided tour spoken by Colleen Moore visitors listen to instruments fixed round the stand.

CHAPTER FOUR

A Twentieth-Century English Stately Home: West Wood House

A childhood memory of Eagle House, Mitcham, Surrey inspired the drawing David West made to show the prospective owner his idea of West Wood House (see page 89). He never uses scaled drawings so it is the only 'plan' he made, preferring to allow designs for the next stage to evolve as he works.

This house is not a large dolls' house, with easily accessible staircase and rooms; West Wood, enlarged to human size, would be a very desirable residence indeed to live in.

As the designer wanted its rooms to suggest different moods this meant they were, like the exterior, a blend of his memories, research and fantasy. To be the architect, builder and interior decorator of a realistic miniature dream house sounds wonderful, but his practical difficulties were enormous. The central parts of the house, for example, had to be finished before they became inaccessible working areas once interior walls were built.

David West's solution was to create all four complete floor areas, build up the ground-floor rooms' walls and repeat the process to the roof. To enhance the realistic effect the thirty rooms' shapes differ greatly and there are five halls and staircases; also, the centre of the house, usually the darkest area, is full of the light descending from the hexagonal dome-topped cupola on the roof.

Once the basement section was finished it was attached to the ornately carved stand, recessed and beaded to form a plinth, which needed to be strong as well for it supports a nine by six feet square house weighing, approximately, five hundredweight.

The roof also has a carved cornice frame to the attic floor; its tiles are carved mahogany and there are two hundred turned balustrades forming the balcony round the cupola, the sides of which are glazed doors.

Four and a half years after starting on the floors he began the exterior walls, which are mahogany, textured and painted to resemble stone. This hard wood was preferred as it has little figuration and is reasonably easy to work; also, being absorbent, it responds well to acrylic paint.

Most eye-catching is the conservatory exterior, formed like an oriel window and hinged for opening. All the window frames are pine, and hand-carving all the glazing bars was, as the maker said with feeling, quite an endurance test.

Some roof sections are removable and the house is open to view on all four sides by means of more than twenty hinged walls. Only the front's centre section lifts off, being held in position otherwise by a brass locking-pin (which is shaped like a mouse) in the attic. Perhaps it is an important mouse in another sense also, for it seems to portray David West's fascinating capacity for combining practical craftsmanship with unusual artistry.

If anyone works on a miniature house for nearly seven years, off and on, it is only natural to feel involved in the project. However, on one occasion West Wood House's maker was involved to the extent he thought it would be, quite literally, impossible to leave the building. Because of the size of the house David West had been working on it in an old barn and one day, while attempting to fix a door in the back wall of the kitchen in the basement, it was necessary to get his head right inside the room to see – with the aid of mirrors – if the quarter-inch hinges were straight. The inevitable happened, he became wedged, his neck muscles developed cramp and no one was near to offer assistance. It was half an hour before he was able to ease himself out again, during which time he had visions of the fire brigade eventually being called and sawing the house in half in order to free him.

Unlike the builders of ordinary houses, makers of miniature ones may not have to ascend dangerous scaffolding, but it seems there are hidden perils for them in the most unexpected places.

DAVID WEST

Sometimes in salesrooms' catalogues a piece is listed as 'the property of a lady' and the phrase will have to suffice in this book as the owner of West Wood prefers to remain anonymous; though she has most kindly permitted the description and photographs of this unusual and beautiful miniature house to be recorded.

Having so often wished that it was possible to ask the makers of antique baby houses how and why they constructed them it was, for me, a rare and exciting privilege to be able to question the maker of West Wood house, David West.

He studied at Camberwell School of Art in London, which he left in 1960, and spent the next twelve years alternately teaching and pursuing ideas about painting and perspective; the use of perspective and its effect always fascinated him.

Later, wishing to experiment with three-dimensional surfaces to paint, he began making decorative boxes and cabinets: for the last sixteen years he has been a professional artist and increasingly involved with designing and making commissioned work.

In 1978 one buyer asked him to create a miniature house; as it had to contain a large collection of miniature furniture and objets d'art the scale had to be one inch to the foot, but apart from that one stipulation, he was free to design what he wished.

West Wood House took seven years to design, build and decorate. Originally he had envisaged it surrounded by a garden with stables and a conservatory, all placed on a large table; but its final position in the owner's home was changed and this plan had to be altered. The house is now placed on its own decorative stand in a corner situation, so the gardens are on shelves behind the house, another visually unusual feature and a surprisingly effective solution.

As the illustration suggests, it is not like a conventional baby house in construction – although its exterior does show its inspiration was an early eighteenth-century English house.

West Wood House was built by an artist, one who could work with wood but who always saw and designed the building as a painter. Unlike a conventional cabinet-maker he had to work from the centre of the house outwards but, in one way, he followed in the footsteps of the early Dutch makers of fine cabinet houses. Like them, he also wanted his miniature house not only to present a harmonious atmosphere within its walls, but to have some affinity with the room in which it was placed, for people to feel West Wood House also has the elements and quality of a fine piece of furniture.

He is constantly 'exploring', and his present commission is a sixteen-foot tall wood carving for Warwick University.

THE CONSERVATORY

The conservatory is the only part of the house which differs from David West's original drawing; then it was seen as a free-standing unit, but it evolved into a deep oriel window, an additional section for the long gallery hall. When closed it hinges on to the raised ground floor of the house, forming a projecting part of the right wall. The scrolls, ornately carved acanthus leaves, are most decorative but their main function is to act as a locking device, using weight and pressure, to support the heavy structure. All the exterior ornamental details, the urns, the scrolls and swags, are carved wood. Open, it affords a full length view of the hall, and the conservatory itself forms one of David West's 'picture book illustrations' in a mahogany frame with sycamore inlay.

The conservatory has a sloping, radiating fanlight, designed in stained glass for dramatic lighting effects which subtly change as the daylight alters. It is interesting to note how often, in a seemingly static construction, the maker manages to create 'moving pictures', in the sense that lighting has been deliberately used to vary the effect of a room or vista.

The exquisite flowers are antique Viennese bronzes and others in the house were made by the owner and the creators of the famous Queen Mary's Dolls' House garden.

THE LONG HALL

Standing facing the long hall the light from the conservatory comes in over the shoulders; but the eyes look towards the other source of light, which descends from the cupola through a balustraded well on the landing above the far end of the hall.

David West is immensely interested in the effect of light shafts in a house and also in the use of perspective; both are particularly important in this part of West Wood. He also enjoys 'framing' interior views; here the side columns are incorporated into the architectural design.

The floor pattern, by a perspective device, draws the attention towards the far wall, where the central door leads into the study. Either side of the door is a niche containing a figure, and it was these two statuettes which determined the depth of the niches and, to some extent, the proportions of the hall.

Thousands of tiny pieces of wood were inlaid into the ground floor's base to make the realistic 'marble' and parquet floors for various areas, and the hall's walls were the first to rise from this base when David West began enclosing the central part of the house.

The chimneypiece was constructed in panels and its position affected the design of the upper storey's rooms.

THE LONG HALL

This is a closer view of the interior of the long hall, but, however closely one looks into it, it is doubtful whether its secret door would be found. (A panel, just by the first door on the right, seen on page 91, opens to reveal a staircase descending into the basement butler's pantry off the servants' hall.) The ceiling is easier to see; David West painted these pastoral scenes on the inset panels, applying the paint directly on to the birch which, together with sycamore, was used to make both ceiling and walls.

Due to the maker's fascination with vistas and lighting (should size permit) it would be possible to stand under the cupola-well and, having opened the doors, look out of windows on all four sides of the house.

The paintings hanging on the walls are the work of West Wood's owner – an involvement which links her to Mrs Carlisle and Princess Augusta Dorothea. (Similarly there is a connection between David West and the designer of the fairy-tale Castle as both chose to 'frame' so many of the rooms in their buildings.)

Some of the fine pieces of furniture in the hall were made by Denis Hillman, a famous miniature furniture maker.

THE SPIRAL STAIRCASE

One of the blessings of a big house is the number of odd spaces which may be used for storing or just leaving things. Beyond the wall is the entrance hall and main staircase; this side a spiral version winds up to the first floor, linking two important areas and also providing several glory-holes. Judging by these delightful dolls it is also an attractive place to play.

For David West the spiral staircase was hard work; first the framework had to be exactly made to measure and then, once the treads and risers were fixed, there was the difficulty of making sure the verticals remained upright during and after any necessary clamping. After it was completed the staircase was dropped into position and secured. David West described the making of this staircase in three words, 'an absolute pain'. The main problem was setting the handrail and balustrade; glue and clamps were essential and, with this small-scale staircase, the clamps hid so much of the structure that it was extremely difficult to even check that it was straight from all angles. The result shows this little spiral is just as fascinating as the splendid main staircase.

THE STUDY

On the left side of the house the principal rooms make a more definite statement in colour than the delicately toned rooms on the opposite side. The hall's centre door leads into an irregularly shaped study; here the warm wood-tones of panelling and parquet flooring, comfortable leather chairs and collector's clutter make it instantly appealing.

At the same time the room provides a complete visual contrast to the cool formality of the beautiful spacious hall. When the door is open there is one of David West's 'paintings' framed in the architrave, a splendid bright vista down the long hall to the conservatory beyond; close the door and the feeling of relaxed comfort in this compact, mellow ambiance is immediate. It is one of those subconscious effects which take much planning to achieve.

The frieze, with a hunting, shooting and fishing theme, simulates moulded plasterwork but it is painted low-relief carving and the entire fireplace, seventeenth-century in style, is also wood; both lighten the room without diminishing the woodwork's warm effect.

On the right, waiting for a gramophone, is a sleeve containing a copy of the record playing 'God Save the King' in Queen Mary's Dolls' House.

THE LIBRARY

The library presents a completely different atmosphere to that of the study; it is elegant and ornate in design and decoration, with a magnificent carved doorway, inlaid floor and 'moulded' (i.e. carved) ceiling. It is a classically proportioned room and suggests Kent's rather than Adam's influence; the white paintwork and natural wood-tones effectively combine with the richly patterned wallpaper to produce a grand effect in a relatively small room.

The wallpaper was actually painted directly onto the wooden walls, and David West also painted the family portrait hanging in a very elaborately carved frame over the fireplace – which is entirely constructed of sycamore.

Boxwood was chosen for the ornamental bows, swags and rondels surmounting the recessed shelves which hold, beside books, some of the owner's collection of miniature porcelain.

As in real life flowers do add immeasurably not only to the visual but also to the emotional appeal of any room; the blooms in decorated containers and the Limoges vase were made by the owner.

Denis Hillman made the corner chair, which is half-hidden by the Pembroke table to the right of the fireplace. This table provides another link with Mrs Carlisle's Rooms as it was made by Fred Early.

THE ENTRANCE HALL

West Wood's front door leads into a square hall with fine panelling, decorative carving and a 'marble' floor, all anticipating the glories within the house itself. The same patterned flooring extends through the ornately carved archway, across the main hallway through to the dining-room door, providing another of the designer's inviting vistas.

Throughout West Wood it was his aim to suggest those viewing the house could 'enter' it without consciously having to minimize themselves; to accept this small scale as they accept a small television image as 'reality'.

It is easy to imagine oneself walking up the splendid staircase, one of the house's principal features. Each of the two hundred and fifty balustrades needed for the staircase and landing had first to be turned and then carved by hand; for this delicate work David West had to use a fine scalpel.

As the staircase had to be formed in situ, and there were so many decoratively carved parts to fit together and angles to be considered, it was a major construction effort.

Nobody could fail to notice this staircase, but there is another one leading from the hall. Hidden behind the door on the immediate right of the illustration a spiral staircase winds up to the first floor.

THE UPPER LANDING

To allow light from the cupola to reach the ground floor two spaces had to be contrived, in the landing's ceiling and floor; and the rimmed hexagonal halo which appears to float above the balustraded space certainly adds a new dimension to the area.

Although the far central doorway leading into the long gallery looks the most imposing entry all the doors from the landing have carved decorative architraves.

Unlike many landings this one is interesting, mainly because of the complex design of the balustraded spaces but also due to the beautifully decorated walls. Above the carved dado and narrow border the 'wallpaper' is apricot, with a pattern which blends in colour with the woodwork surmounted by a swagged design embellished with gold. As usual in West Wood the walls were painted, but here the design has been screen-printed.

Both the fine table and chest are modern, made by Denis Hillman, although the table holds some lovely old glass candlesticks and porcelain jars.

The two playful puppies on the rug (made by the owner), the Dalmation and the ferocious kitten on the bannister rail are all painted Viennese bronzes. The owner also painted the landing's pictures, except for the landscape above the table.

THE LITTLE DRAWING ROOM

This most unusual room is in the front of the house, to the left of the door. As in full-scale houses certain rooms have their shapes determined by the need to fit in a staircase or passage on that floor, and so it is in West Wood. Also, the designer was constantly evolving interesting interlocking visual patterns, as well as vistas, within the house.

In this morning or small drawing room the ceiling is the most dramatic feature, with a central ornamented area framed by a deep, carved cornice to the main level.

Its striking effect is emphasized by the room's irregular walls, with their 'wallpaper' and dado providing more eye-catching details. The room's colour scheme and the clever use of contrasting friezes unite what could have been most awkward shapes to balance.

There is a mixture of furniture in the room; a delicate, tall ivory bookcase against the back wall, with a black 'lacquer' long-case clock and bureau nearby, contrasts a little oddly with the less delicate definitely dolls' house chairs grouped round the low table.

However, even in the stateliest of real houses one finds a blend of period and 'comfortable' furniture in rooms not open to the public, and this room certainly presents an interesting and intriguing mixture.

THE DINING ROOM

Another beautifully panelled room, with a considerable amount of fine carving to suggest its early eighteenth-century influence, is the dining room. Here the wood used is ash, so the effect is much lighter than that of the mahogany panelling in the study and entrance hall.

The room is at the back of the house, so the elegant doorway with its high, carved pediment opens onto the long hallway, with the study to the right. With the door open there is another framed vista right through to the front door beyond the entrance hall.

For the intricate inlay of the patterned floor, pine and mahogany were used; the ornately carved fireplace, with painted marble surrounds and Dutch tiles, and the overmantel were constructed of sycamore. In this room the cornice is very elaborately designed and deeply carved.

David West particularly enjoyed designing the service hatch: usually it is hidden behind his Dutch inspired painting of parrots eating their food, but the picture has been raised in its frame to reveal the hatch.

Both alcoves were mirror-lined and shelved to display more porcelain miniatures. The superb chairs and dining-room table are the work of two famous contemporary miniature furniture makers, John Hodgson and Denis Hillman.

THE NURSERY

Nurseries in years gone by were always as far removed as possible from the rest of the house, for 'children should be seldom seen and never heard'. Happily the West Wood children seem to have the run of the house, from the basement to the attics where their nurseries are traditionally sited.

The mansard roof sections and the dormer windows, edged with birch mouldings, lift off to reveal a suite of rooms, which have plain pastel-coloured walls and polished wood floors.

This day-nursery has a positive toy-shop of playthings with a rocking-horse, tiny toy-theatre, dolls of all kinds, a toy fort and a wooden push-along horse, in fact a really fine collection of modern miniatures which are small-scale for dolls. To the lonely little inhabitant of the bleak, ornate attic 'nursery' in Sara Ploos van Amstel's house (page 63), the comfort of this nursery under the eaves would seem as amazing as the variety of playthings on the floor.

Next door the night-nursery, in addition to its usual items of furniture which include a pretty lace-trimmed Victorian cradle, has a realistic white polar-bear rug on the floor; following the pattern of the antique baby houses it also has a trimmed baby-basket on the floor for all the infant's accessories.

THE MASTER BEDROOM

The master bedroom in West Wood House is in the front of the building and its colour-scheme relates in much softer, paler shades to the deep apricot and mahogany tones of the landing beyond. In this room the decorative, charming setting provides an interesting contrast to the somewhat dark and rather heavy pieces of furniture.

Except for the fragile shelved stand by the fireplace, which holds more examples of the owner's miniature porcelain, the dressing-table and stool, bedside bookcases – with more porcelain – and the massive four-poster bed all, in every sense, stand out from their felicitous surroundings.

In due course no doubt the bed will have curtains and quilt to complete its comfortable quality for the owner of the shoes, though then the kittens may have to find another place to sleep.

Again, these murals were painted directly on to the wood, in this case birch ply, before being assembled for the room's construction.

They have a soft, dreamlike quality – and perhaps the landscape is in Serendip, for the flock of sheep are grazing conveniently near the bed for easy counting on sleepless nights.

THE CHINESE BEDROOM

This lovely room, over the long hallway on the right of the house, continues that side's pale effect with its mural of soft blues and white, and touches of pale apricot and warm wood-tones to link it to the landing's deeper colouring.

All the patterns have a Chinese theme and the unusually situated fireplace is one of the most imaginative in the house; each successive 'frame' radiating outwards from the grate makes it, although not centrally placed, the focal point of the room.

David West said he envisaged the house as a three-dimensional picture-book and this is another of his framed illustrations.

The fret-edging of the external wall-opening colour-links with both doors and the low Chinese table; and the design ornamenting the dado and architraves relates to the more complex interwoven pattern of the frieze.

Although, strictly speaking, not the focal point, the ceiling, carved in deep relief, is certainly eye-catching. Its swirling Chinese design provides the irregularly shaped bedroom with a touch of grandeur.

Unlike the furniture highlighted, the little bed does not have quite the same affinity with its surroundings – despite the canine guardian at its foot.

Like Mrs Carlisle, West Wood's owner stitched most of the modern carpets, this rug being a splendid example.

FURNITURE

There can be no question about the suitability of the furniture placed against the wall, and the Chinese landscape mural provides a perfect background for these black 'lacquer' pieces with finely painted gold designs ornamenting each front section. In Vivien Greene's notes, sent from her Rotunda Museum of antique dolls' houses, Oxford, she records that this furniture was made in the 1930s by 'a Mrs Birkbeck, who did all the decorative painting, Miss Cross and some local schoolchildren'.

The products of this cottage industry, which was continued by Miss Cross after Mrs Birkbeck's death in 1936 until she herself died in 1940, were sold at Morrells, in the Burlington Arcade, and in the Medici Galleries, both in London. All the furniture's cupboards open, the desk's to reveal pigeon-holes and drawers.

The imitation cane-and-lacquer chairs and settee perhaps betray their origin more obviously, but they are interesting and inventive examples of handcrafted dolls' house furniture.

Although all the specimens in West Wood – there are more in the little drawing-room – are black lacquer, the same pieces were also painted green, cream and red.

There is only one piece of authentic Chinese furniture in the room – the delicately carved, low square table in front of the fireplace, but it blends in very well, helped by the beautiful miniature examples of oriental porcelain.

WINDOW DETAILS

It is all too easy to be so absorbed by the magnificence of the house that even when looking at it room by room some small, but most important, details escape notice. This window in the master bedroom is a fully working sash-window, made exactly as a full-size one would be with a properly jointed frame and glazing bars of pine wood. All the panes are 2oz. glass, not perspex. This particular window also has an attractive blind fixture.

As West Wood has thirty rooms it was an undertaking just to make this set of fixtures. In addition to these ordinary windows two features needed extraordinary ones. The conservatory has, under its stained-glass fanlight, ten long eight-panel windows, each with a smaller four-panel window set above and hinged to open. The hexagonal cupola has sides made as a set of glazed doors, jointed to decorative corner posts. Its dome, incidentally, was shaped in pine and lined with mahogany, and all the dormer window frames are ply, with birch mouldings.

No wonder their maker described the windows' construction as quite an endurance test.

THE GALLERY FLOORS

Throughout the house David West used perspective to create the extra effect he wanted from a particular space. He began making the house by designing all the floor areas, and here the use of perspective is clearly seen. Once you know what to look for, when properly applied, the means do not intrude into the end effect.

Over six thousand tiny pieces were used to make the 'marble', parquet and board floors in West Wood, and all had to be individually cut. This was due to the need for the pieces to be inlaid towards the far walls to be fractionally narrower than those for the front area of the floor – a perspective 'trick' to suggest greater depth. Boards were always laid parallel to the opening and were reduced in width for the same reason; diagonal designs, stressing corners not sides, were also used. A rug was removed to illustrate this and we see how the fireplace tiles were cut to increase this illusion.

The mantelpiece, fireplace and grate are painted wood for the 'metal' parts; box, holly or walnut was used, alternately painted and sandpapered then, finally, honed with holly to create a sheen.

THE LONG GALLERY

The long gallery on the first floor of West Wood extends across the entire back wall of the house and the illustration opposite shows the left-hand side. It is a magnificent room, with finely carved and panelled mahogany woodwork and a bordered inlaid floor as its most obvious attractions. The particularly fine double-doorway is set in a recessed area off the central section of the gallery and is a most imposing entrance to this splendidly proportioned room.

All fifty of the interior doors were made with mortice and tenon joints and panelled; they were then hung in position with quarter-inch brass hinges, glued and pinned.

Visually the gallery separates into three sections, the outer two having a fireplace as their focal point and the central section relating to the doorway. It is also interesting to see how the ceiling has been carved to relate to the floor, geometrically, whilst it connects in colour to the fireplaces and, of course, sets off the rich shades of the panelling.

The still-life paintings are the work of the owner, and the tapestry over the right display cabinet is by Jennifer Gunnings. Most of the porcelain is Limoges, the owner having made a fine collection of these miniature pieces before West Wood was built.

THE LONG GALLERY

The photograph below was taken to illustrate not only the right side of the long gallery but also to show how, by looking through its central window (on the left of the illustration), a long vista through the house connects it to the middle window of the façade – provided the doors are open first of course.

Inside this section of the room is the pair to the other fireplace and against the right wall stands a particularly fine secrètaire, which was made by John Hodgson.

It seems rather odd for the parlour-maid doll to be cleaning the grate – perhaps she is intended to be showing the housemaid how it should be done. Nevertheless, although both dolls are charming, they do make one wonder at what period in the house's history we are looking.

As West Wood is, very obviously, a home as well as a superb house, a mixture of period furniture is most appropriate, but perhaps the most effective clothes for the occupants would be modern ones; however, this is a debatable point.

All the furniture in the gallery is of fine quality, but the musical instruments are perhaps the most eye-catching.

THE KITCHEN

As is frequently the case in reality one of the most important rooms in any house – the kitchen – is in the basement. It may have a (painted) stone floor and a lower ceiling than those upstairs but there is a very generous amount of space in which to work, judging by today's standards.

Unfortunately the splendid AGA cooker, made by Basil Smetham, is partially hidden by the big chopping table. Exciting the appetite of the kittens on the floor below is a fowl, one of the many examples of the astonishing range of realistic miniature food created by modern craftsmen; another example is being eaten off the floor, apparently to the wrath of the parlour-maid doll.

She and the seemingly unperturbable cook were both made by Jill Bennett – more of her dolls are illustrated and described in Chapter Six.

Certainly the dolls and animals do add to the appeal of this kitchen; for, however well-equipped such rooms may be, without these characters kitchens can seem just to display a collection of cooking utensils rather than to be an integral part of a realistic household. (To illustrate this point one only has to refer to Nostell's kitchen on page 136).

In designing West Wood's kitchen David West carried on the time-honoured custom of providing almost unreachably high shelving for the shining saucepans brightening up the basement room. Like all good traditional kitchens this one has white paintwork and plain blue walls – that colour being generally chosen in the belief that 'blue repels flies'.

The realistic stone paving forming the usual floor surface may appear cold, but it was, in theory anyway, easy to keep clean (although such an opinion might not have been shared by those who actually had to scrub the kitchen floor as a daily task).

David West made the splendid old-fashioned kitchen table with its large working-surface, here almost covered with mixing-bowls, bottles and dishes. Also the long dresser, taking up most of the right wall; it has good-sized, opening, drawers and cupboards, and shelves to support the fine assortment of kitchen equipment displayed. Both these pieces, like the chopping table, are unpainted wood.

The basement, served by its own back-stairs into the butler's pantry and a secondary staircase, also contains several fascinating utility and store rooms.

CHAPTER FIVE

Miniature Rooms: The Thorne Rooms and The Carlisle Rooms

Parallel to the ever-growing enthusiasm for dolls' houses shown by adults during the past three decades is the increasing fascination for fine miniature items felt by a much smaller, but equally dedicated, number of collectors. This second group is not usually attracted by commercially made dolls' house furniture, however well produced; for their purposes it is necessary to have perfect small-scale replicas of antique furniture, ornaments and furnishings in order to create the desired realistic effect in their miniature rooms. Few, if any, would aim to equal the achievements of two of the best known collectors in this field. Mrs James Ward Thorne and Mrs Frederick M. Carlisle, as both collections are truly outstanding.

It is interesting that, as for the miniature house, the period 1920 to 1940 was the miniature rooms' most splendid renaissance to date. Also intriguing is the realization that two creative collectors, one in the United States and the other in England, should be engaged in establishing their important collections of miniature rooms over approximately the same period of time, but quite independently of each other. They might seem to be running on similar tracks, but there are distinct differences, as well as more subtle ones, in their approach to the subject; although, at first glance, the rooms themselves might seem sometimes to belong in either collection.

In the first part of this chapter the spotlight is focused on the American collector's rooms as, although Mrs Carlisle also began collecting at the turn of the century, the settings for her miniatures were not made until some thirty years later. By that time Mrs Thorne had begun exhibiting her first series of rooms to the general public.

There are sixty-eight Thorne Rooms now in the Art Institute in Chicago: thirty-one in the European Set (which, for the purposes of display, has been expanded to include a Chinese and a Japanese traditional interior) and thirty-seven in the American set.

When Mrs Thorne presented her gift to the Museum in 1940 she included the first set she had made; but this series was sub-sequently sold by the Museum to the IBM Corporation who arranged for them to tour America for several years.

Sad to relate her son, Niblack, found some in a bad state of repair, but still on display, in a New York store some twenty years later. IBM and Mrs Thorne generously had them restored (many needed complete refurnishing also) and the Corporation then presented sixteen of the original set to the Phoenix Art Museum in Arizona and nine others to the Dulin Gallery in Knoxville, Tennessee – the other five rooms were dismantled. Thorne Rooms are now on display in three museums in the United States.

Mrs Thorne set up a fund, in 1954, for the care of those placed that year on permanent exhibition in the Art Institute of Chicago, to whom she also gave over 500 drawings, blueprints and notes on the rooms. Over thirty people worked in her studio creating rooms which were furnished with a combination of antique and modern miniatures. Mrs Thorne stressed that the series did not depict the history of interior design, but only presented some important influences.

As Mrs Thorne was American it seemed appropriate to concentrate on her third series of rooms as they focused on interior decoration in the United States, and exemplified the influence of European styles upon American designers. There is an earlier (1799) hallway, but my choice of this 1835 entrance hall, based on the hall in The Hermitage, near Nashville, Tennessee, was due to the fine pictorial wall covering.

Mrs Thorne, as we know, did not imitate exactly any particular room; here she chose to use a wallpaper, in the style of one in The Hermitage, but actually owned by the Art Institute. The original wallpaper, 'The French in Egypt' was made in 1814 by Dufour, the French firm specializing in scenic wallpapers.

The hall's furniture is in the popular mid-nineteenth century classical style and the console and table designs were based on pieces in The Hermitage, the home of Andrew Jackson, twice President of the United States.

MRS THORNE

Mrs Thorne, then Narcissa Niblack, was born in 1882, to the wife of a well-established businessman living in Vincennes, Indiana. In an age when such daughters were expected to become gracious wives and hostesses, cultivating social graces took priority over educational prowess; but she was fortunate enough to travel extensively with her parents, at first to the East Coast cities then across the Atlantic. In Europe she was greatly influenced by the stately homes and castles they visited and her keen appreciation of architectural and interior decoration was developed as she began to discover which period and style she preferred.

In 1901 Narcissa Niblack married a childhood friend, James Ward Thorne, one of the four sons of the wealthy co-founder of Montgomery Ward and Company. All the brothers were involved in the firm and James became vice-president and director. His early retirement, when only fifty-three, enabled him to indulge in more travel and photography.

They had two sons, Niblack and Ward, and their position in Chicago society involved her in both cultural and charitable work. Even so, the Thornes travelled extensively, which enabled her continually to add finer and more beautiful pieces to her collection of miniatures – begun in her childhood when a naval uncle kept sending home tiny things from stations abroad.

During the Twenties a childish enjoyment of dolls' houses developed, by serious study, into a daunting ambition: the creation of a series of miniature rooms all aimed to display the most important and influential styles in European and American interior decoration.

There have been many speculations about her inspiration for these rooms; it seems most likely she was influenced by three more or less coincidental things. Mrs Thorne found a miniature room-setting in the form of a shadowbox on her travels in Turkey, shortly after she had been forced, by the accumulation of miniatures at home, to rent a studio to store some items.

At the same time an increasing number of important American museums were exhibiting full-scale period rooms, which, in turn, influenced fashionable, wealthy people to have at least one room in their homes either recreated in period with imported antiques, or designed to imitate that effect.

Mrs Thorne decided to have a series of small rooms made to display her miniatures to their best advantage and use them to illustrate some important highlights in the history of interior design.

Thirty of these Thorne Rooms were shown publicly at the Chicago Historical Society in 1932 in an exhibition to benefit the Architectural Students League, for Mrs Thorne maintained an interest in charity work throughout her life. Twelve months later they were exhibited again in a building specially designed for them at Chicago's *Century of Progress* exposition. As hundreds, then thousands of people queued to see them Mrs Thorne was encouraged to start an even grander project, an inch to the foot scale set of thirty rooms, with specially commissioned furniture, to present a chronological 'History of European Design'. It was, however, to be a purely personal selection and her reasons for choosing these rooms reflect her own preferences.

This set was completed in 1937 when the indefatigable Mrs Thorne began a third series, this time to illustrate American interior decoration. Again her choice of styles was entirely her own, and this set was finished in 1940.

All three sets were made for educational as well as display purposes and completed her project. Mrs Thorne, however, continued to create miniature rooms and shadowboxes for the rest of her life, although these were single settings complete in themselves, and made as gifts for relations and friends.

It is particularly interesting that these 'unofficial' rooms and street scenes were the only ones to be inhabited by human figures and even by animal characters from Beatrix Potter's tales.

The shadowboxes were also sold in aid of charities, and the last two rooms she made were for the Children's Memorial Hospital in Chicago. These were completed and presented not long before she died in 1966, aged eighty-four.

AN ENTRANCE HALL

In complete contrast to The Hermitage Hall, both in style and period, is this 1751 Entrance Hall, closely based on the one in Carter's Grove, James City County, Virginia; here the fine panelling of the hall and staircase has been left unpainted.

The house which inspired this model had all the wood-carving supervised by Richard Baylis, an Englishman who came over especially for this work. The man who was most deeply involved in the production of all the American Thorne Rooms was Eugene Kupjack; in every one of these thirty-seven settings there is at least one piece of his handiwork.

He was a young man during the time he worked for Mrs Thorne; when the project was completed he was inspired by those years to start a miniature-making business of his own. Today he is regarded as one of America's finest miniaturists.

As much of the needlework seen in the rooms comes from the same source it is likely this carpet was ordered from the Needlework and Textile Guild of Chicago. Founded in the mid-Thirties it produced many commissioned pieces, for collectors and other interested people, and Mrs Thorne, appreciative of their high standard of needlework, ordered several items.

VIRGINIAN DINING ROOM, KENMORE

The lighting of this room and the Entrance Hall adds greatly to their atmosphere: this room needs full sunlight to display the delicate plasterwork of the ceiling and the fireplace panel to best advantage.

This room is called 'A Virginian Dining Room *c.* 1752' and its inspiration is given as Kenmore, Fredricksburg, the beautiful Georgian brick home of George Washington's sister, Betty, after her marriage to Colonel Lewis. It is very noticeable in this setting that the inspiration has been substantially altered on Mrs Thorne's drawing-board to provide the blueprint for this miniature room.

She was more interested in stressing the main features of Kenmore than in reproducing with complete accuracy any one of its rooms, and in suggesting the ambiance of the time and place rather than recording its actual layout. Here, the fireplace panel is from Kenmore's library, the doors on the back wall have altered positions, and the windows have been adapted into door windows.

The furniture also has been modified or, in the case of the gilt-framed mirror, added to – the chains from eagle to urns are not on the original version.

The miniature silver should be noted; made by John Moore, it came from Tiffany's.

VIRGINIAN DINING ROOM, GUNSTON HALL

Many fine eighteenth-century Virginian mansions were designed by Englishmen and Gunston Hall in Virginia is a good example. William Buckland designed the house for George Mason, who named it after his ancestral home in Staffordshire.

Gunston inspired Mrs Thorne to create this Virginian Dining Room, 1758; however, although the house as originally decorated had been the first in Virginia to have rooms decorated in 'Chinese style', these particular designs were added by another owner in the late ninteenth century.

As this room at Gunston initially had white walls with all woodwork, including the dado, painted yellow, one might prefer Mrs Thorne's version to an authentic copy.

The fret, often used in Chinese and 'Chinese Chippendale' furniture, features as a decorative design on the doorways, windows and overmantel and also on the serving table, sideboard and chairs.

Two oriental statuettes surmounting the far doorways, the elaborate gilt-framed 'Chippendale' mirror and the carpet add to the rather strange mixture of patterns in the room, though the delicately designed wallpaper on a pale blue background is charming.

The attractive silver hides a secret: both tureen and basket have Liberty dimes as bases and the wine coolers French centimes.

JEFFERSON'S VIRGINIAN DINING ROOM

In this Virginian Dining Room, *c.* 1800 Mrs Thorne wished to pay tribute to Thomas Jefferson as a classical architect and inventor, and also to illustrate an important French influence – the Empire style.

The plain turquoise walls and white woodwork effectively emphasize the delicate crystal and gilt wall-lights and chandelier, the gilt-framed medallions and the elaborate ornamented mantelpiece with its decorative gilt overmantel.

Through the archway – a device Mrs Thorne often used to suggest the perspective she required – is the famous 'tea room' extension of Monticello. Just visible on brackets are two of the four plaster busts of Jefferson's heroes: George Washington,

Benjamin Franklin, the Marquis de la Fayette and John Paul Jones.

Mrs Thorne has recorded three innovations credited to Jefferson: the folding glass doors, a ventilation device – by dividing the windows into three sections – and a most ingenious panel in the mantelpiece which connects with the wine-cellar.

She also included a miniature copy of Thomas Jefferson's own dining-room table. The other Empire examples in the room were replicas of exhibits in various museums; the crystal chandelier and delicate pieces on the table are particularly beautiful. Even the needlepoint rug was copied from a French design in the Empire style to complete the effect she desired.

NEW HAMPSHIRE DINING ROOM

Mrs Thorne chose to illustrate the styles she believed to have most inspired or dominated American interior design. Many of the rooms are based on those from eighteenth-century East Coast states, as these were the ones upon whom transatlantic influences had the greatest effect.

In this 1760s room she displayed an imported French scenic wallpaper – though its peak of popularity was a hundred years later – and American versions of English furniture designs, sometimes called Colonial Chippendale. The carved shell-shaped corner cupboard holds a fine little collection of miniature versions of Chinese export pieces – the carpet also has an oriental pattern.

An unusual touch is the placing of a hatchment over the fireplace; this side of the Atlantic it would usually be displayed, after the death of a family member, outside a house or, later, in a church.

The soft colouring of the room is typical of its period and, although its shape and proportions are not the regular ones Mrs Thorne preferred, the whole effect is very pleasing.

This room was based on one in the Wentworth-Gardner house, Portsmouth, New Hampshire, a building usually regarded as a perfect example of an American Georgian residence.

Pale apricot brocade curtains and fine miniature silver pieces provide the lightening touch the other muted tones required.

WASHINGTON'S VIRGINIAN PARLOUR

The shape of the Virginian Parlour, dated 1758–87, makes it seem an unusual choice for Mrs Thorne with 'her overwhelming passion for symmetry'. However, the asymmetrical west parlour at Mount Vernon, George Washington's home overlooking the Potomac River, was the inspiration for this room

Small though it is it has some imposing features: the Palladian-style doorway and the pedimented fireplace wall; the windows also, by the judicious use of long, draped curtains, are made to appear more dignified.

A special feature in many rooms is the chandelier; this is a good example of the heavier crystal type.

George Washington imported a great deal of furniture and furnishing from England after his marriage to Martha Dandridge Custis and Mrs Thorne had several replicas made for this room where the Washington arms surmount the fireplace pediment.

The General's portrait is partially visible through the doorway to the rear room – Martha Washington's silver tea-tray and the Aubusson carpet presented to her husband were also copied.

Some suitable furniture in museums has been copied also, but this delicately coloured little room is a delightful, if surprising, one to be so strongly influenced by George Washington.

NEW YORK CITY PARLOUR

A 'New York City Parlour 1850' was Mrs Thorne's intention when she examined Theodore Roosevelt's reconstructed house on 28 East 20th Street for ideas.

The features Mrs Thorne decided to illustrate were a fireplace and overmantel, the ornamental cornices in most of its rooms and the fashionable blending of many patterns in one room.

It must have been difficult for her to present all these in one room as she had, according to Eugene Kupjack, 'an overwhelming passion for symmetry'; to combine the fussiness and overdecoration the period required, while achieving a balanced effect in a room uncluttered with furniture, seems almost impossible.

Her solution was to take the typically patterned wallpaper, another patterned carpet, ornate rococo furniture, gilt mirrors, books and ornaments and fit them into a setting designed to suggest a spacious room with elegantly draped symmetrical windows.

The two cloisonné vases on the consoles are antiques, but the furniture was specially made. All the books were finely bound and the one on the round marble-top table actually contains a readable copy of Lincoln's Gettysburg Address.

As the rooms, like stage-sets, lack a fourth wall, placing furniture realistically without obscuring the view of the pieces against the back wall is particularly difficult.

COUNTRY PARLOUR

As one might expect, the Country Parlour is double the size of the town one; but, of course, only by clever use of perspective through the archway as the second 'half' is only an indication of the room itself.

Although of the same period as the New York City Parlour, this room appears old-fashioned; compared to the up-to-date many patterned town house parlour it seems far more gracious and attractive.

The main features of this type of house were high ceilings, decorative plaster mouldings on cornices and mantelpieces and the use of arches rather than doors to allow air to circulate through these Southern rooms.

This room is labelled 'Georgia Double Parlour 1850', the decade prior to the Civil War; Mrs Thorne's notes reveal that she used the bay window from a *Gone with the Wind* film-set as the inspiration for this miniature version.

In this bay is a 'chaperone' seat, one orginally designed to prevent a couple sitting too close to each other.

Georgia had been an English settlement and there are many English touches in the room: a Wilton carpet, the circular tables, the wax fruit under a glass shade. The chandelier provides a dramatic focal point for this elaborate room.

MASSACHUSETTS DRAWING ROOM

In this representation of a 1768 Massachusetts Drawing Room Mrs Thorne has linked it to England in two ways. Her inspiration was a room in Jeremiah Lee's mansion in Marblehead, New England, which had a wood-panelled parlour, richly carved after the English style; he also imported much of his furniture from England.

Mrs Thorne's room is probably more elaborately furnished than Jeremiah Lee's, but she was aiming to convey the ambiance of that time rather than to reproduce exactly a particular room.

The pieces she chose to place in this setting were mainly Queen Anne in style, and the two finest were made by the London firm of cabinet makers and antique dealers, Arthur Punt – who also supplied Queen Mary with specially made miniature furniture in addition to antique pieces.

Arthur Punt made the long-case clock, which can be opened and wound, and the superb writing-bureau of burr walnut. All the drawers in this exceptionally fine piece are removable and it also has a secret compartment.

The needlepoint carpet was copied from an English design by members of the Chicago Needlework and Textile Guild.

One striking difference between this room and the panelled room opposite belonging to the Carlisle Rooms, is that all the Thorne Rooms, unlike the glass-topped Carlisle ones, have proper ceilings, from which hang the lighting fixtures, often rather important features in this series.

QUEEN ANNE DRAWING ROOM

This is the first of the Carlisle Rooms, one of Mrs Carlisle's favourites as it was the work of a much admired craftsman, F. J. Early. He provides another link between the Thorne and Carlisle Rooms for he made miniatures for both series. He also created items for Titania's Palace and Queen Mary's Dolls' House and was regarded as one of the foremost miniature makers of the 1920s and 1930s.

This taciturn Sussex craftsman made all the furniture in the Queen Anne Drawing Room – the first Mrs Carlisle commissioned, in 1933. All the drawers have dovetailed joints, the locks turn and the beautiful writing-bureau has several secret drawers.

Mrs Carlisle valued his work so highly that, in 1968, she had this new room-setting of Parana pine specially made as she did not feel the original setting was quite worthy to hold his superb miniatures.

The porcelain is Limoges, but the figurines on the mantelpiece are the work of the multi-talented Albert Reeves.

Apart from the double chair and stool seats, which were made in Vienna, Mrs Carlisle made all the chair-seats, the fire-screen and the carpet.

In this series, with one exception, the scale is one-eighth throughout.

MRS CARLISLE

Katherine Apcar was born in Calcutta in 1891. She attended a convent until her parents sent her to England to be educated at Roedean, a bracing Sussex school better known for games than the fine needlework which became her absorbing interest.

After a stay in Paris in April 1914 Katherine Apcar married Frederick Montague Carlisle M.C., then serving with the Northumberland Fusiliers. He left the army in 1924 and became a Lloyd's Insurance broker, so their first real home was in London until the War. Later they moved to Wiltshire then in 1946 to Pyt House, Ashampton, Berkshire. Mr and Mrs Carlisle had four children, three sons and a daughter, Diana.

Mrs Carlisle was given some miniature silver furniture in childhood; these were finally housed in the glass cabinet she found in 1934, with walls specially painted to represent Chinese eighteenth-century wallpaper. (Tragically it, with nearly twenty-five percent of her collection, was stolen in 1972, from Greys Court, near Henley after she had given the rooms to the National Trust.)

Although they were always her private collection, the rooms were shown to the public occasionally to aid charities.

She left Pyt House in 1973 moving to Aynhoe Park, Northamptonshire and, finally, to her daughter's home where she died in 1979; like Mrs Thorne she, too, was an octogenarian.

Besides the rooms Mrs Carlisle had many interests: gardening, bridge, the National Trust and collecting (treen to military badges), but, always, her main interest was needlework. All her homes had beautifully made patchwork quilts, tapestry chair-seats and cushions, and the rooms always contain her work.

A WILLIAM AND MARY PARLOUR

This William and Mary Parlour, made in 1959, shows not only Mrs Carlisle's Savonnerie carpet and set of chair tapestries but a miniature example uncompleted in its frame, and it is interesting to compare this version with the full-scale one in the photograph of Mrs Carlisle on the page opposite.

Both setting and furniture were made by Horace Uphill and the silver miniatures are antique Dutch, the 'pictures' German enamels and the alcove figures Chinese.

The wall mirror and baby-walker were the work of Albert Reeves, an invaluable craftsman who with immense versatility made many items for the rooms.

Miniature-making was a childhood hobby for him; wartime service with the Metropolitan Police and managing an instrument works afterwards left him little free time, but increasing commissions became a full-time occupation until ill-health limited it again.

He was equally skilled in woodwork and ceramics, but the piece he was proudest to have made was always the spinet in the Music Room.

ADAM MUSIC ROOM

DETAIL OF THE ADAM MUSIC ROOM

The set of tiny Japanese instruments inspired Mrs Carlisle to plan this Music Room in 1960 and she commissioned Albert Reeves to make the Adam-style setting and furniture.

He used Wedgwood jasperware, originally designed for brooches and rings, as wall-plaques and table decoration, modelled the portrait busts and then, having finished the wall-sconces to complete the setting, he started on some of his finest work, the spinet and cased violin – he also made the conductor's baton and music-stand.

It seems unbelievable but they can be 'played'; at least, a sound is heard when the violin is bowed and the spinet strings may be seen to be correctly plucked when its notes are pressed.

Both mandolins were made by a pupil at Beccles School and Mrs Carlisle stitched the stool and chair-seats and the carpet.

The harp, cello, another violin and a viola da gamba were created by a Welsh craftsman from Cardiff, John Thomas. The beautiful Welsh holly harp has a double action pedal movement and forty-four strings, an amazing feat as it required a hundred and seventy-six holes to be drilled to hold them correctly.

Unusually, creating the miniature harp caused him to become one of only three professional full-size harp makers.

DETAIL OF THE REGENCY GAMES ROOM

Like the Music Room this Regency Games Room also evolved from a box of miniatures Mrs Carlisle wished to display; tiny chessmen, backgammon pieces, dominoes and cards, even dice are arranged here on tables made in 1953 by Horace Uphill, a cabinet maker and furniture restorer in Wilton and Salisbury.

Apart from Albert Reeve's chairs, Horace Uphill made all the inlaid tables, bookcases, even the brackets and fireplace for the setting D. B. Waterhouse ARIBA designed.

The pictures are Baxter prints and American whittled flowers fill the alcove urns in the passage. On the mantelpiece the silver-gilt lidded bowls are Georgian in design but were made in time to be stamped with a Coronation hallmark.

Mrs Carlisle's needlework is particularly noteworthy as, in addition to the Axminster carpet, bell pull and striped chair seats, she made the perfect little games-boards, all in petit point.

In 1925, Horace Uphill 'drifted into' making miniatures when, unable to find the travellers' samples an American customer requested, he offered instead some he had made. By 1933, he was working on pieces for Titania's Palace and then in 1952, after a television appearance, for a real queen, Queen Mary, who was another constant miniature-collector.

REGENCY GAMES ROOM

CHIPPENDALE LIBRARY

The Chippendale Library, made in 1934, is another room mainly furnished by F. J. Early. His mahogany desk is a small masterpiece, with drawer locks which actually work. The carving on two of the chairs shows his ornamental skill and the drumtop table, on page 8 and break-front bookcase emphasize his care in using the wood's grain to the finest advantage.

It contains some lovely eighteenth- and nineteenth-century editions of French and English books; there are over fifty miniature volumes including a copy of the Koran and Gita, a 1770 almanac, and Queen Elizabeth II's Coronation broadcast text.

Between the bookcase and desk is a long stool with a pair of unfolding library steps rising from the seat which normally contains them. The unusual framed maps are dated 1599 and 1615. Mention must be made of the delicate painted metal flowers often arranged in the rooms; here some tulips are just visible on the passage table – these were made by Evelyn Nicholson.

The Persian carpets, of course, are Mrs Carlisle's work. She had a Visitors Book, partly seen on the table, specially bound by Sangorski and Sutcliffe to contain signatures of all the craftsmen involved in the rooms' creation; a similar volume holds the Carlisle's family photographs.

NURSERY

Not all the rooms are as splendid as the Library opposite – Mrs Carlisle had a greenhouse, an antique shop, even a toolshed in her collection. But all, including the sparse 'utility' post-war Living Room were exquisitely made – there were 1,600 beechwood blocks in the 1951 Living Room parquet floor, for example.

As has been mentioned elsewhere, Mrs Carlisle's rooms reflected her interests so, as her grandchildren were born, she created two modern nurseries.

Albert Reeves made the second, the Night Nursery in 1961, partly to take the overflow of toys from the Day Nursery, which was constructed by R. Magna and J. Moore in 1955.

The setting and much of the furniture were made from a sycamore in her garden at Pyt House, but the toyshop of playthings, antique and new, came from many countries. The procession of ivory animals, heading for an ivory ark, were specially made in Africa and brought home by her daughter and a son. R. Magna and J. Moore made the dolls' house and fort, and the rugs, of course, are by Mrs Carlisle.

The framed panels are little eighteenth-century cut-outs, made by two children at that time; 'here ends Fanny's and begins Mary's', the tiny writing informs us.

GEORGIAN BEDROOM

Looking at the Georgian Bedroom, and even knowing it was a blend of antique and modern (1954) craftsmen's work, it is almost impossible to distinguish between the two.

The partly visible linen press, filled with embroidered linen in ribbon-bound piles – the gift of a Women's Institute (who also gave the tatting) – has a very thick 'false' front which might betray its age, but the other pieces are confusing.

R. Magna and J. Moore were responsible for the modern replicas, but their bed's quilt and cradle's coverlet were made by Averil Colby. Other antique pieces are the corner washstand, chest and mirrors, cheval glass, bedside-table and cradle. The pictures are Baxter needlecase prints and the fine carpet was made by Mrs Carlisle. R. Magna, then a Royal Engineer in the British Army, was drafted into making models for the D-Day invasion preparations. After the War he founded a model-making firm in Fulham and Mrs Carlisle heard of him through the Council of Industrial Design for whom he made model furniture. J. Moore joined him in 1949; having also been a model (ship) maker he was already an expert in miniature work and continued as Works Manager when, aged only forty, Mr Magna died in 1959.

PALLADIAN HALL

This is the last of the Carlisle Rooms, made betwen 1964 and 1966 and, were it not for the label 'Palladian Hall', the photograph would appear to illustrate the entrance to a full-scale stately home.

It is unusual, for it is the only one in the collection to portray a cross-section of two floors and only the second to be closely representational of an actual room.

As Mrs Carlisle had not created a hall before she chose to base one on the entrance to Hatch Court in Somerset, a mid-eighteenth-century house designed by Thomas Prowse.

The indomitable Albert Reeve not only constructed this miniature model but also made every piece of furniture it contains. Having designed and made a half-inch-to-the-foot cardboard model he used it to work out all the construction details before beginning the setting itself. He carved by hand the prototype for the delicate balusters and then the necessary eighty-four replicas were cast.

Only after they had been fitted into the staircase framework could the twenty sections of carved wood for the double handrail be jointed together to complete this section of the hall.

On the next page the furnishings are discussed in more detail.

DETAIL OF THE PALLADIAN HALL

The dramatic effect of the hall is enhanced by the striking 'marble' floor pattern – one of the two alterations of the original's design, for in Hatch Court itself the floor is polished wood.

The other deviation is the inclusion of the miniature portraits, tiny replicas of the Dring full-scale paintings of Mrs Carlisle's grandchildren.

She herself was one of the rooms' finest artists for almost all the needlework they contain was her own work. The two oval carpets and the stair-carpet in this hall are quite an achievement for, to suggest the proper effect of a carpet pile, Mrs Carlisle threaded her needle with two lengths, one of silk and one of finest wool (using two tones for each colour) in order to achieve this realistic result.

For the hall alone, eighty-eight inches of bordered stair-carpet and the two rugs were stitched employing this method, a feat which shows not only Mrs Carlisle's considerable skill but her dedication.

The two panels hanging either side of the windows are not painted but stitched; they are embroidered tapestries, designed by Frances Kay and twenty-eight threads to the inch were needed to produce these detailed architectural views.

MRS THORNE AND MRS CARLISLE

Although they never met or corresponded there are some interesting links between Mrs Thorne and Mrs Carlisle. From an early age both collected miniature objects, a hobby which developed into an absorbing fascination in later life.

Both collectors employed the finest craftsmen of their time, blended commissioned and antique pieces and designed rooms which, though faithful to the style and period illustrated, were usually based on certain aspects of real rooms rather than as accurate miniature replicas.

Having decided dolls would distract from the realistic effect they desired, both left it to the viewers to decide whether to imagine, from clues provided by the miniscule personal possessions, the rooms' unseen occupants, or whether to imagine themselves living in the rooms.

They did differ greatly though in their approach to collecting and in the way they envisaged their rooms' development. Mrs Thorne was, in a sense, almost a professional collector. With an organized team of workers under her personal supervision and a definite aim – to reproduce in miniature, aspects of the history of interior decoration for museum presentation – the creation of her rooms increasingly affected the way she lived.

The way Mrs Carlisle's rooms originated, however, was entirely different as what she saw, did and collected inspired and influenced the making of each individual room, which she designed to be a unit. She is shown below with one of her earliest rooms.

There was no long-term plan into which rooms had to be fitted; this series evolved, often by chance or a sudden idea. For instance, the Regency Room was made to house her collection of miniature games, some small Japanese musical instruments led to the creation of the Adam Music Room, and the Nurseries were made after her grandchildren were born; every room in the Carlisle series has a very personal reason for its existence.

CHAPTER SIX

Dolls from the Seventeenth Century to the Present Day

All the rooms in the last chapter are unoccupied, and their contents are perfect miniatures of the fine furniture, ornaments, carpets and curtains which attract so many people to full-size stately homes. It is hardly possible not to admire them, not to wonder at the skill of all the craftsmen and women involved.

Admiration and praise are well deserved and fascinated viewers almost invariably pay due tribute. With one's mind registering both appreciation and wonder perhaps it is absurdly ungrateful to wish unoccupied rooms also had the power, without inhabitants, to touch the heart. However, given the unlikely choice of receiving as a gift the unoccupied Titania's Palace, or a good miniature house, complete with kitchen, family and animals, my decision would not be very difficult to make; the Palace is wonderful to visit and admire, but the other would be welcomed and cherished, the warmth of a 'home' being preferred to the sterility of a 'museum', however full of precious objets d'art.

Why? No doubt psychiatrists could supply various theories, but perhaps the most convincing reason is the simplest one; rooms are in houses, and houses are homes and people live in them.

Could it then be said all miniature houses should be occupied by miniature people and pets, in other words dolls?

As usual, nothing is that simple. If the doll is unsuitable because of its making, clothing or size it can ruin, completely, the effect of any room. The more correct the miniature inanimate objects surrounding it are, the more abrupt the disappointment and irritation of the viewer if the doll does not match up to their standards.

Most of this chapter's photographs illustrate occupied rooms from famous antique houses. Do the occupants increase or destroy the effect of miniature realism? Does their presence heighten the impact of a room's atmosphere or destroy it? Is their clothing appropriate, and do they look like display dummies or real people wearing it?

The following pages show some of the ways dolls have been used by collectors; perhaps if the illustrations are looked at with these questions in mind, some answers may be found which will surprise the reader.

This room in Petronella de la Court's late seventeenth-century cabinet house in Utrecht's Centraalmuseum, though obviously a richly decorated salon, depends considerably on its occupants to enhance its stylishly elegant atmosphere. With this group of unusually naturalistic dolls the room appears 'alive'; they convey the suggestion of conviviality enjoyed in splendid if not luxurious surroundings.

All these dolls have beautifully modelled wax faces and well-proportioned bodies – if their posture appears unrealistically stiff to our eyes, perhaps the tight corseting of men and women, necessary for such a splendid appearance, might be to blame!

Both their wigs and elaborate costumes are fashionably French in style; so also, judging by a 'La Bourée de Basque' score on the double music stand, is their musical taste. They seem a group of talented amateur musicians, playing flutes, violin, cello and clavichord.

Apart from a console table, bearing the blue and white porcelain usually found in fine Dutch houses, and a brocade-covered table laden with wine glasses, the chairs are the room's only furniture; all have the popular astragal style legs and stretchers and are upholstered in brocade matching the tablecloth.

The wall paintings are of Italian landscapes by Frederick de Maucheron, whose canvases were usually full size. With these fine dolls in such a room, no wonder the effect is charming.

A MALE COOK

Contrasting vividly with the richness of the Dutch music room is this kitchen in Nostell Priory, the miniature house in the stately home of the same name, now in the care of the National Trust. Made *c.* 1740 it is one of the most famous of all the eighteenth-century English baby houses.

The sole inhabitant of the kitchen is a male cook – chef being a later term – and he does look rather unrealistic in these surroundings. Apart from that regrettable stand he would enhance the look of his kitchen – and its low doorway would not appear such a hazard; unfortunately, despite his immensely interesting attire, he does lessen the intended effect.

The enormous treble-arched fireplace, with side-ovens, is surmounted by a complete spit-rack and winding-gear fixed to the stone-painted back wall. There is the usual unreachably high shelf for jars and a most unusual plate-rack, standing not hanging, but alas, no food. On the floor by the table, between the chair and the chopping block, there is only a minute ivory mouse.

Despite the kitchen's appliances it lacks the appeal and realistic effect of Nostell's splendid reception rooms – though it is immensely interesting as a record of domestic implements.

Empty-handed, with nothing to cook, no wonder this lone occupant looks morose.

A FEMALE COOK

Of the same period as Nostell Priory's kitchen, this second one is in another superb baby house, again still in its stately home, Uppark, also administered by the National Trust.

As at Nostell, the attention is drawn first to the items in the kitchen rather than to the room as a whole – which is hardly surprising as it contains over seventy pewter plates, ranged along and piled on the shelves, besides the shining pots and pans brightening the stove and table and even needing floor space to hold them all.

Amongst this splendid assortment are some more unusual items: ivory cutlery, a box-iron, a candlebox and a rare machine for making chocolate.

Although the table and chairs befit the room many of the implements are far too large for it. Like Nostell, this kitchen is a curious mixture: here, an attempt at realism seems unaffected by any need to match scales.

Cook, female this time and more informally dressed than at Nostell, is a pleasing wooden doll, with, it is thankfully recorded, a good-sized capon and pies to prepare for a meal.

Both dolls are unrealistic, but this one definitely adds charm and warmth to the room's atmosphere, which contrasts favourably with Nostell's rather sterile appearance.

UPPARK SERVANTS

In 1845, according to Charles Dicken's book *The Cricket on the Hearth*, there was a distinct social hierarchy in England's doll society as well as in the real world: those representing the upper classes were made of wax, the middle classes had leather bodies and 'the common folk were wood'.

Although these rigid rules were not always observed it would seem such class distinction was of long standing; both the dolls in the two rooms on these pages were installed there over a hundred years before Dicken's book was published.

The wooden doll has an unusually well-carved head and hands, and is dressed in the style of livery such as a real servant might wear in a similar house of that period. He and his fellow footman, coming through the second door, are in the fine first-floor dining room of the Upprk baby house.

Like the kitchen in the same house – on the preceding page – Upprk's dining room has a problem over differing scales. Were it not for three things, the dolls, the over-large brass door furniture and the candle-sconces either side of the elaborate fireplace, it would be hard to determine whether it was the dolls' house or a real room. It also appears that the cook and the footmen might be related as all of them have the same shaped head and hands.

BLACKETT FAMILY DOLLS

The architecturally realistic miniature house given to the Museum of London by Mrs Blackett, is another well-known example of a fine, mid-eighteenth-century English baby house.

Its four main rooms behind the magnificent façade are less impressive. This small withdrawing-room conveys a sense of gracious living in an elegant age, despite the disparity between the over-sized dolls and hand-painted wallpaper pattern and the smaller scaled dado and mantel-less fireplace.

The playing-card screen, upholstered chairs, mirrors and circular table are all in scale with the original room; gilded moulding was added later, rather spoiling the true eighteenth-century effect. The hand-made carpet is also a later addition. More to the dolls' scale are the ornaments, goblets and pretty lute.

Made of wax as befits their status, these original dolls in their deceptively simple silk dresses and turbans languidly recline, as far as this is possible on such chairs.

Eighteenth-century English miniature house-makers, who would have been commissioned especially by their wealthy clients, sought to make their work resemble full-size façades; but the houses' interiors and dolls were not generally required to look so realistic.

NURSE AND CHILD

When the famous fine English wooden dolls, Lord and Lady Clapham, were saved from exile abroad their wardrobe of outer and undergarments provided costume researchers with much useful information.

It is very seldom that the smaller dolls' house dolls can provide such hidden details, but what is visible of this doll's costume is interesting and identifies her as being from the Waterlands district of the Netherlands. Underneath is a set of beautifully sewn underclothes.

All the dolls in this house, once owned by Petronella de la Court and now in Utrecht's Centraalmuseum, are exquisitely dressed, – as fashionably as the music room group on page 134 – or in regional costumes; unlike contemporary English dolls, all these are life-like.

Probably modern children will feel more pity than envy looking at the child-doll, so sensibly held by long leading-reins. The full-length dress may be beautiful, but it is only part of an outfit as stiff and richly ornamented as any adult's. The elaborate bonnet must have been both tiresome and uncomfortable to wear at that age and the poor infant appears to be almost as tightly laced as her nurse.

NURSES, MOTHER AND BABY

Like the nurse in charge of the toddler the two women in attendance on the mother and newborn baby in the lying-in room wear their regional costumes. The attention to detail in all the clothes is remarkable; although the three nurses look similarly dressed there are noticeable variations of sleeves and head-dresses.

The dolls throughout the house have beautifully modelled wax heads and limbs giving them a most realistic appearance. Particularly noticeable is the wet-nurse holding the swaddled baby; her breast has been permitted to appear uncovered for obvious reasons – a rare pose and surely one of the most touching and delightful arrangements to be found in a miniature house.

The draped bed is comfortably positioned in an alcove, but the rest of the room seems too fully-furnished until one remembers all the visitors expected to congratulate the mother.

The fragile ivory chairs and the equally delicate statuettes and cabinet carvings emphasize the importance of this panelled room; and with a fine collection of porcelain vases on display, and two tables with trays laden with a tea-set and dishes of food to refresh the visitors, the effect is both elaborate and intimate.

DINGLEY HALL OFFICERS

Eighteenth-century German and Dutch dolls' house occupants, as a general rule, tended to look more realistic than English ones, but by the late nineteenth century many dolls in English dolls' houses at least had fairly realistic heads, although their limbs and proportions remained doll-like.

This fine pair of Hussar officers in their splendidly colourful uniforms may not look entirely natural – the one in the red jacket would have to be at least seven feet tall – but their faces, either bearded or with a moustache, look acceptably realistic. The doll wearing the green jacket and shining helmet is better proportioned than his companion; his uniform has finer details and his properly sheathed sword looks more authentic.

They are on the central upper landing of Dingley Hall, now in The Bethnal Green Museum of Childhood, London. Both the original owners and their house are unusual as it is rare for teenage boys to show interest in miniature houses. Dingley Hall was made for the Currie boys in 1874, when the hobby of the elder brother Laurence, who collected miniature things, expanded into filling this fourteen-room house, which is over nine feet wide.

With two male owners it is hardly surprising that most of the dolls in the house are male also; most are from Germany originally and many are costumed in various Hussar uniforms.

DINGLEY HALL STAFF

Dingley Hall is a fascinating house, one of the few to have its own private chapel, complete with two officiating priests.

Laurence and Isaac Currie, though probably unwittingly, followed in the wake of Sara Ploos van Amstel for they, too, had a notebook in which they kept a record of items bought for their hobby house.

One priest, they note, was bought, undressed, 'for one and sixpence in the Lowther Arcade', a wonderful establishment off the Strand in London where, in the 1870s, children could walk down aisles of toy and doll stalls; they also note the necessary vestments for the doll were 'a gift' from their mother.

More attractive dolls are seen throughout the house. Though not so spectacular as the Hussar officers, or as elegant as the female members of the family, nevertheless the household staff at the Hall are an interesting group.

Maids, most of whom wear fetching little ribbon-trimmed caps, fichus and aprons over their dresses, are bisque-headed German dolls, as are the chef and bootboy. All wear suitable and beautifully sewn costumes, perhaps more 'gifts' from Mrs Currie.

ENGLISH NURSERY DOLLS

The most fascinating thing about these dolls in Ann Sharp's baby house is that, three hundred years later, their tiny handwritten identity labels remain pinned to their original clothes. They stand in a room often called a nursery, although it was originally probably a lying-in room – the misleading pasteboard dolls' house is a later addition. Its magnificent bed, with embroidered green silk curtains, and a fine walnut cradle. inlaid with ivory, are typical of the impressive ones found in lying-in rooms.

'Sarah Gill, ye childe's maid' and possibly the baby's, is the well-dressed wooden doll looking towards a large silver posset-pot near another lying-in room item, the trimmed baby-basket on the floor. 'Ye childe' doll, resplendent in a hooped yellow satin dress is wax, like the baby, but only to her waist; to stand she has to rely on her stiff skirt.

These dolls are in the earliest recorded furnished English baby house, made about 1695 and given to Ann Sharp by her godmother, the future Queen Anne.

Unlike the superb seventeenth-century Dutch cabinet houses, this is a plain six-foot high cupboard house, with a storage shelf above its nine rooms.

It was a rare gift at that time, even for an Archbishop's daughter, a child's plaything and not a display case for an adult's miniatures. Even so, it contains an interesting mixture, in scale and value, of fascinating items.

GERMAN NURSERY DOLLS

The dolls in this room were added some time after the original house was built in Germany, at about the same time as Ann Sharp's cupboard house.

Although the English one contains some good pieces it was a plaything; in this splendid German example, now in the Nationalmuseum in Nuremberg, everything is of fine quality for display.

The house itself, first owned by the Kress family, is an odd mixture; basically it is a display-cabinet, with turned balustrading across all the rooms and landings. Some years later, in the eighteenth century, it was altered and given additional gables to make it appear more 'realistic', although the rooms still remained permanently visible.

Dolls were installed also and both they and their clothing equal the quality of the furnishings throughout the house. The beautifully dressed doll holding the wax baby doll, swaddled in the continental manner, also has a realistic wax face – in striking contrast to her linen arms and extraordinary hands with fingers of tiny strips of linen, tightly rolled and sewn.

This room has been rearranged several times; now a completely natural-looking baby doll, wearing only a shift and a bib, sits in a highchair in front of a well-stocked linen-cupboard which gives an authentic nursery touch to this room – though the well-laundered bed linen is very elaborate for a nurse's bed.

'DOWNSTAIRS' DOLLS

This is a tastefully decorated *salle à manger* in an interesting dolls' house, with a realistic exterior, given to the Musée des Arts Décoratifs in Paris, by Madame de Presle and described as French *c.* 1850.

With a 'marble' mantelpiece, and heavily draped window curtains matching the dark green fabric-covered walls above the dado, it could look rather dull and sombre.

The furniture's arrangement adds to its formality and the chairs against the wall suggest an old-fashioned owner/occupier.

It benefits from some bright touches: an elegant glass chandelier and matching pair of candelabra, pictures, mirror and gilt overmantel all lighten the room's effect.

More unusual and delightful are the birthday cake with lit candles, for the little girl in the next room perhaps, and a fascinating glass goldfish bowl on a metal stand under the window.

This is not an ordinary goldfish bowl, for it has as a centre piece a branch of coral with a green plant 'growing' beside it in the simulated water.

Standing in the centre of the room is a black-haired china-headed doll, her costume suggesting she is staff not family. Are her stance and position accidentally as stiffly formal as the room itself? One cannot laugh at her, but she does raise a smile, perhaps, as the question is pondered.

'UPSTAIRS' DOLLS

This is another upstairs room in the same well-furnished house which, though it is also an elegant reception room, conveys an atmosphere totally unlike that of the old-fashioned arrangement of the formal green dining room.

It is certainly accidental that all the pictures do not hang tidily in a straight line on the crimson silk-covered walls, but the three little occasional chairs have been deliberately and unaccountably placed in the middle of the room, and this contrasts oddly with the previous room's very precise arrangement.

In addition to the Waltershausen chairs, settee and escritoire, the salon has two gilded metal three-shelved chiffoniers with various ornaments, including a pair of casserole-shaped flower containers, and two circular tiered tables, an ivory one with tripod legs and a gilt metal one.

Placing well-dressed dolls so informally in a far corner, and allowing a poodle into the salon, attracts not only the eye but also the imagination. Has the visitor put her feet up to gossip with her hostess? Is the room's rather disorganized appearance due to a recent party, or, perhaps, a domestic crisis? Without these dolls the salon would seem to be just an untidy room, but with them it can offer additional pleasure by intriguing the viewer.

MADAME DE PRESLE'S COOK

It is unlikely that this narrow, windowless little room would have been considered a very realistic representation of a mid-nineteenth-century kitchen; it might seem more like a ship's galley were it not for the two attractive upholstered red wooden chairs.

It does, however, contain some pleasing and even rather interesting items. There is a functional looking cooking-stove, complete with copper pans, and on the wall next to it is a white sink, with a fitted pipe and a big brass tap; this is an unusual feature to find in a mid-nineteenth-century dolls' house; generally the tubs beside the fixture would have been considered sufficient. The doll, taller by far than the others in Madame de Presle's house and generously proportioned, to put it politely, seems even larger in such cramped and congested surroundings.

As she is, literally, singlehanded, reaching the array of china and glass on those high shelves or unhooking any of the saucepans would appear to present quite a problem.

It is curious that someone displaying such interest and taste in the decoration and furnishing of this house should be content with the occupants' appearance; charming though they are the dolls do not match the quality of the furniture. Perhaps they were the only ones she could find and her interest in fine sewing did not equal her fascination for interior decorating.

MADAME DE PRESLE'S HOUSE

As the kitchen is wedged in between the spacious ground floor salon and the dining room of equal size it is possible that what was once the entrance hall has been made into the kitchen that this dolls' house originally lacked.

As the exterior view of the house shows, the front door (with its imposing surrounding portico) seems disproportionately large for this little two-storey building. Inside, the width of the door is the entire width of the back wall of the hall. While this is perfectly adequate for a hallway, especially when there is no staircase for it to contain, it does present difficulties when adapting the space to provide a kitchen.

In fact Madame de Presle's house presents us with several odd inconsistencies apart from the lack of a staircase (a common dilemma for many doll inhabitants) and that peculiarly unsuitable kitchen. For example, the house's exterior looks realistic and each room, with the exception of the unfortunate kitchen, has a side as well as a front window. Heavy draperies may obscure the view from the windows but they are properly glazed and have ornamental ironwork outside, strong enough to provide good protection on the ground floor.

However, though the rooms have lighting and fireplaces none of them has a door . . . an irritating and puzzling omission.

MADAME DE PRESLE'S DOG

How enviable to have not one but two rooms in the same house with sets of profusely decorated black 'lacquer' furniture. This bedroom's opulent look is largely due, of course, to the superb bed, draped with crimson silk, fringed and tasselled to match the curtains at the arched window. With similar silk covering the footstool and seats of all the chairs, save the one partnering the dressing-table, the room has a rather pleasing and harmonious, if lavish, effect.

As in the other room, this furniture appears to greater effect because of the contrasting touches. The delicate ivory, or bone, workbox on a stand (also with matching touch of crimson) is but one of three indications that the occupant enjoys needlework; the other two are a metal workbox on legs on the right and a polished wood tapestry frame by the bed. Perhaps the round table's well-stocked tray is of some significance too.

The chandelier pairs with the one in the peach salon but, although the walls are similarly covered, this room has a blue-grey dado to enhance the colour scheme.

No doll is necessary to enliven this bedroom, the trespassing Pomeranian (or is it a chow?) capably manages this entirely alone.

AMATEUR MUSICIANS

The 1850s house once owned by Madame de Presle boasts two equally well-furnished salons; unlike every other room in the house this one has no dado. With peach silk-covered walls, soft blue curtains, touches of blue on the glass chandelier and blue goblets on a little ivory 'drinks table', its colour scheme is most pleasing. It certainly provides an excellent background for the room's chief attraction, the set of black 'lacquer' furniture which is copiously decorated with vividly coloured flowers.

The ivory chess table and fragile metal plant-stand look particularly delicate by contrast, and the filigree firescreen with a painted landscape blends in beautifully. The red salon's chairs merely look irritatingly untidy; here, because of the mandolin's position, a similar trio immediately suggests a musical evening.

Both dolls do more than suggest; their positions, leaning against the piano and reclining on the settee, inform the viewer that performing is a tiring occupation. A doll like the settee's exhausted young occupant usually spoils any realistic effect, but here perhaps not. In those days children were told not to put their feet on the furniture, however tired they felt; possibly this doll reminds us she has not forgotten her manners.

EIGHTEENTH-CENTURY DOLLS

This unusual set of rooms is also in a French museum, the Musee des Arts Décoratifs in Paris, described as 'early eighteenth century, possibly Spanish or Portuguese'. It is difficult to fit it into any category; though it hardly qualifies as a miniature house it is more than a room setting.

The little 'cabinet' is almost over-decorated, without and within; its salon, with so many patterns, ten ornamental pillars, gilded frieze and mirror, looks curiously amateur in design, and the furniture is an interesting mixture too.

The murals do not reveal its nationality as the one in the dining room depicts Pisa's Leaning Tower, and the salon has Germanic and Italian landscapes, also a marine panel of sailing-ships in a stormy sea – surely an unsuitable choice for such a delicate room.

There are more puzzles: why does the Chinese influence only affect the roof; and why, when there are no doors, windows or fireplaces, is a table so realistically laid and laden with soup tureen, food and six bottles of wine?

The seven dolls definitely add to its mystery; they are realistically painted and dressed as befits their station – the family in kneebreeches and silk gowns, the servants in plain or peasant-style costumes, and all are sufficiently well jointed to enable them to sit or stand in reasonably natural positions.

GRODNERTAL DOLLS

There is nothing puzzling about the early nineteenth-century dolls' house at Audley End in Essex. Apart from its rather basic exterior, and the distressing, but not unusual, lack of any staircase within, it is a delightful, well-furnished house, partly a toy and partly a decorative collector's item.

Dolls in this residence are not confined within box-like compartments; all ten rooms have one, two or even three windows each and most have fireplaces and intercommunicating doors.

The largest room in the house is this sumptuously decorated gold and crimson reception room on the first floor, where one doll is placed at her harp with three companions seated ready for the recital.

Although the house is famed for its tin furniture this drawing room is furnished with sofas and chairs upholstered in crimson silk and probably home-made like the footstools and matching, seemingly wind blown, gold-edged crimson curtains, with deeply swagged pelmets over the three large windows.

It also has some fine pieces: the silk-panelled pianoforte, an interesting horn table, three gilt-framed mirrors and, above all, the rare and delightful white and gold harp with tiny painted flowers as decoration.

The well-dressed musician and her audience are Grodnertal dolls, the little jointed variety beloved by Princess Victoria.

BISQUE-HEADED DOLL

There are two rooms en suite in a dolls' house which was given anonymously in 1958 to the Musée des Arts Décoratifs in Paris and it is interesting to compare their furniture with the set in the house which belonged to Madame de Presle (illustrated on pages 142 and 143). In that home the black 'lacquer' pieces are lavishly decorated with ebullient flowers and gilt designs, suggesting the head of the household had expensive and rather opulent tastes.

Here, although this furniture is also flower-ornamented and gilt-trimmed, the opposite effect is achieved and all is sweetness and light. The white furniture, the childlike, almost innocent, look of the doll, the pale pink shades of the upholstery, walls and carpet all add to the pretty, unsophisticated effect.

The bedroom is even more suitable for this little doll as it has a pastel flower-patterned wallpaper, white furniture matching the salon's suite, and a little gilt looking-glass and a glass goldfish bowl on a stand as the only ornaments.

These small, jointed bisque-headed dolls do present a problem to dolls' house owners as, although not all were meant to be children, their proportions and facial expressions do not convey easily an adult effect even when they are costumed as fully-grown men and women.

The little glass-eyed example opposite could have been dressed to suggest a small child or a *jeune fille*; but her pose, and her short skirts, would be more acceptable on the former and produce a better 'natural' effect in this rather sedate, though prettily decorated room.

A communicating door connects this salon, which is double the size, to the adjoining bedroom. As both rooms have the same style of furniture the whole of the first floor presents a unified picture, although the bedroom's upholstery and drapery are pale blue not pink satin. Similar central medallions ornament both ceilings, and crimson, brown and gold freizes are colour coordinated with their wallpapers.

The windows in both rooms are lace-draped, and the one on the left in the salon leads to a pretty little balcony over the front door.

Of particular interest is the instrument in the far right corner as the gilt-edged pink panels and 'scraps' decoration are not usually found on such pianos.

A pair of jardinières on either side of the room have been carefully planted with a regard to colour as the flowers blend in attractively with the room; so, also, do the candles in their gilt candlesticks. Most of the ornaments, the mirror and ornate clock for example, are gilded too and add considerably to the salon's attraction.

TWO DOLLS IN COLLES COURT

Colles Court, a large ten-roomed house in my collection, was altered in the 1920s for its late owner to have a 'modern' dolls' house to play with; its original date is uncertain as it is not a commercially made dolls' house.

This study, in which two dolls and their puppy are standing, was constructed in the front half of the old kitchen when the dolls' house was modernized, wired for electricity and entirely repapered – only this room was 'panelled'.

Its furniture is a mixture of crudely made playthings and more interesting items; the early wireless set with head phones, for example, which is between a bookcase and the desk on which a 'daffodil' telephone is standing.

By the brass fender is a rug, a miniature one given away with cigar boxes at that time, and above on the high mantel shelf are two equine statuettes of heavy, painted lead. Books, newspapers, a drinks' tray and an armchair all suggest a comfortable sanctum.

Both dolls have very realistic faces and are typical of the 1920s–30s period; the man doll is jointed and commercially made of a hard, early plastic material painted a peculiarly virulent shade of apricot – his clothes, however, were original models, hand made especially for him.

Elsewhere are two Siamese cats, a kitten and another puppy, but this one always stays close to his master.

MERCHANT DOLL IN FLIERDEN HOUSE

As the Flierden baby house is now a blend of eighteenth- and twentieth-century craftsmanship it is necessary to know a little of its history to understand the reason for the combination.

In the mid-eighteenth century 27 King Street, King's Lynn, Norfolk belonged to a Dutch merchant, who lived there with his family and used some rooms for business purposes.

The Flierden's only child, Ann, owned this six-roomed house, which has, as its front, a replica of her home's façade. Ann died young, in childbirth; her baby house has a shrouded history until the 1920s when it was given to a Children's Society Home in Devonshire.

By 1984 the house needed complete restoration, having lost all its furniture; the Society invoked the assistance of Vivien Greene, whose Rotunda Museum of dolls' houses near Oxford is internationally famous. Mrs Greene, helped by a group of collectors, undertook the task and raised money to refurnish the empty property with suitable, commissioned pieces.

The dolls also are made by contemporary artists, 'the merchant' in his counting house room was created for Flierden House by Jill Bennett.

The restored baby house went on temporary exhibition at Powderham Castle, Devonshire after its return to the Society, who can give details of its present whereabouts.

TWENTIETH-CENTURY DOLLS

Nowadays those who anguish over the question whether or not to include dolls in miniature and realistic-style rooms, are better served than many of their predecessors for a number of talented artists are creating very natural-looking miniature model dolls.

Two of the best known English makers in this field are Jill Bennett and Charlotte Zeepvat. Jill Bennett trained as a theatrical designer, and she combined her love of the theatre with her other great interest in children's book illustrations to create what she describes as 'three-dimensional story-telling characters'.

She loves designing characters with a 'fairy-tale' quality; although she does design life-like dolls as well. These two are obviously the gardener and the mistress of the house in disagreement, apparently, about the length of a vegetable marrow. Both dolls are 'specials' from her J Range: these are dolls designed by Jill Bennett and produced by her with the assistance of a team of expert doll makers and dressers.

Like many more of her dolls the merchant in the Flierden baby house was a commissioned personality, but these two below are Jill Bennett's own choice of character.

The woman doll, with her late 1920s hairstyle and clothes, was costumed by a team member, Jan Clarke. Like all these model dolls she and the gardener have jointed metal bodies and limbs with painted ceramic heads.

The group of dolls at the studio for wedding photographs opposite were made by Charlotte Zeepvat, the doll artist who designs, makes and dresses all her creations so they are entirely her own work. Although best known amongst collectors, here in England and abroad, for her one-twelfth scale dolls' house dolls, she originally chose to make dolls of a larger size.

As a child she was interested not only in having dolls but in finding out how they were made. When asked how her dollmaking career began she recalled a childhood holiday when she was given a Cornish Fisherman doll and felt impelled to dismantle it, discover its construction and then begin making her own designs.

She began specializing in miniatures when the owner of the first specialist shop for dolls' house collectors saw photographs of her work and asked her to create small-scale dolls for her customers.

Since then many of her dolls, like the ones in this wedding group, have been commissioned by collectors, particularly in the USA. The natural appearance of these exquisitely jointed dolls is as much due to their beautifully made clothes as to their finely painted expressive features and extremely delicate hands.

Charlotte Zeepvat's own preference is for seventeenth-century costumes; however, most collectors request the Victorian styles so well represented in this final photograph.

PHOTOGRAPHIC ACKNOWLEDGEMENTS

The publishers are grateful to the following for kind permission to reproduce

The Art Institute of Chicago. © 1990. All rights reserved pp. 110, 113–122.

Frans Hals Museum, Haarlem pp. 44–5.

Caroline Goodfellow pp. 21, 24, 32–3, 40–41.

Diana Gray pp. 124, 133.

Gemeentemuseum, den Haag pp. 52–3.

Musée des Arts Décoratifs, Paris, pp. 152–3.

Museum of London, p. 139.

Museum of Science and Industry, Chicago, p. 68.

The National Trust pp. 125–132.

David West pp. 86, 88 (photo: John Drysdale), 89, 105–7, back jacket.

West Wood House's owner p. 98.

SELECT BIBLIOGRAPHY

Art Institute, Chicago, *Miniature Rooms*, 1983: *The Thorne Rooms*, undated.

Boehn, Max von, *Dolls*, Dover Publications, 1956.

Carlisle, Christopher, *My Own Darling; letters from Montie to Kitty Carlisle*, Carlisles Books (in assoc. with the SPA Ltd), 1989.
Carlisle, Mrs Katherine, *Miniature Rooms at Pyt House*, 1962
Centraal Museum, Utrecht, *Het Utrecht's Poppenhuis*, undated.
Christie's sales catalogues.

Desmonde, Kay, *Dolls and Dolls' Houses*, C. Letts 1972.

Earnshaw, Nora, *Collecting Dolls' Houses and Miniatures*, Collins 1989.
Eaton, Faith, *Dolls in Colour*, Blandford 1975; *Doll's House Furniture*, Shire (forthcoming 1990).

Gemeentemuseum, Den Haag, *Een rondang door het poppenhuis*, a museum publication.
Girouard, Mark, *A Country House Companion*, Century Hutchinson 1987; *Historic Houses of Britain*, Peerage 1979; *The Victorian Country House*, Yale. revised ed. 1979.
Goodfellow, Caroline, *Dolls' Houses*, HMSO Books 1974.
Greene, Vivien, *English Dolls' Houses*, Batsford 1955; *Family Dolls' House*, Bell & Son 1985.
Gröber, Karl, *Children's Toys of Bygone Days*, Batsford 1928.

Herold, Gottfried, *Die Schrippenfee*, Berlin 1985.
Holme, C. G., *Children's Toys of Yesterday*, The Studio Ltd 1932.
Hughes, G. B., *Collecting Miniature Antiques*, Heinemann 1973.

Jackson, Val, *Dolls' Houses and Miniatures*, John Murray 1988.
Jacobs, Flora Gill, *A History of Dolls' Houses*, Cassell 1954 and 1965; *Dolls' Houses in America*, Scribners 1974.

King, Constance Eileen, *The Collector's History of Dolls' Houses*, Hale 1983; *Dolls and Dolls' Houses*, Hamlyn 1977.

Latham, Jean, *Dolls' Houses; a personal choice*, A & C. Black 1959.
Leber, Wolfgang, *Die Puppenstadt Mon Plaisir*, Museum of Arnstadt Publications 1986.
Low Frances, *Queen Victoria's Dolls*, Newnes 1984.

Marwitz, Christa vonder, *Das Gontard'sche Puppenhaus*, Historiches Museum Frankfurt am Main 1987.
McClinton, Katherine, *Antiques in Miniature*, Scribner, 1970.
Museum of Art & Science, Chicago, *Colleen Moore's Fairy Castle*, 1964 and 1981; *The Dolls' House of Colleen Moore* 1949.

Pettit, Sheila, *The Collection of Dolls' Houses at Wallington Hall, Northumberland*, Frank Graham 1975.
Phillips sales catalogues.

Rijksmuseum, Amsterdam, *Poppenhuizen* 1967.

Sothebys sales catalogues.
Stewart-Wilson, Mary, *Queen Mary's Dolls' House*, The Bodley Head 1988.

Thornton, Peter, *Authentic Decor; the domestic interior 1620–1920*, Weidenfeld 1984.
Toller, Jane, *Antique Miniature Furniture*, Bell 1966.

Victoria & Albert Museum, *Dolls' Houses*, HMSO Books 1974.

SELECT BIBLIOGRAPHY

PERIODICALS

English: *Dolls' House World; International Dolls' House News*
American: *Dolls; Doll Reader; Nutshell News*
French: *Polichinelle*
German: *Puppen und Spielzeug*

LIST OF ILLUSTRATIONS

LIST OF ILLUSTRATIONS

INDEX